To Andew

Thank you for your Support

Much Love

WHY?

The Biography of John Carlos

With CD Jackson, Jr.

[signature]

68 + 2001

Published By
Milligan Books, Inc.

Cover Design
By Anthony Moore

Formatting By
AbarCo Business Services

CONTENTS

Acknowledgements

We begin by giving thanks to our Creator God, the One in whom we trust, for without Him our lives would be in vain. To the Carlos family: John's father; the late Earl Carlos Sr.; his mother, Louise Vioris Ward-Carlos; his two brothers Earl Jr. and Andrew; and his two sisters, Doris and Hepsey. Much love and appreciation to John's children: Kimmy, the late Trevion, Malik, Winsetta, and Shana. Special thoughts also go out to all of his relatives and friends. Sincere thanks to the contributions that his late wife Karen made in their marriage. John says that she stuck with him through thick and thin. And to his present wife "Charlene" whose love, strength, business savvy, hard work, and constant devotion lifted him, making his prior days of darkness seem like a microcosm. Much respect and admiration goes out to Mrs. Seneca his grade school teacher at PS 90 Elementary School in Harlem. She had a great influence on John's life. Special appreciation to Jerry and Ethel Williams, Hollywood producer Milan Tiff, sports historian, Urla Hill, Dr. Kirk Clayton, Lawrence Fan (San Jose St. Univ.), Coach Peyton Jordan, and George Carty. All of your many John Carlos stories were excellent. To all John's friends from Harlem: Louie Houston, David Scott, Wally Bowen, Eddie Ellis, Kareem Abdul Jabar, Larry Willis, and Buddy Williams. To the Olympians: Leon Coleman, Barbara Ferrell-Edmondson, Jesse Owens, Wilma Rudolf, Ron Freeman, Wyomia Atus, Ray Brown, Edith McGuire (the beautiful sister who inspired John to run the 100 and 200 yard dash), Willye White, Coach Stan Right, and Jimmy Hines. To the people of Trinidad who gave John his first international trip in track and field. To coaches

Ed Leavy Joe Yancee from the New York Pioneer Club. To detective Lester and Bryant for making John understand that he had a talent to run. To Dr. Paul Grafton from Palm Springs High School who gave John the opportunity to work. To friends Charlie Mayo, John Mayo, and Warren Edmondson. Special thanks to Professor Jan B. Lawson and Dr. Katherine Kreuter from College of the Desert. They both read and assisted with general editing. Their support was invaluable. Much love and thanks to my brother, Principal Thadddus Jackson, who read and gave me constructive criticism. And again, we give thanks to our Heavenly Father who makes all things possible. Straight ahead!

About The Author

C D Jackson Jr. was born in South Central Los Angeles (Watts), California. He progressed through L.A.'s K-12 school system, graduating from David Starr Jordan High School with athlete recognition. After graduating, he matriculated to Angelina College in Lufkin, Texas, on a full basketball scholarship. After attending one year at Angelina College, he relinquished his scholarship, and consequently he matriculated to College of the Desert (a two year community college), in Palm Desert, California, where he earned an A.A. degree in Business Administration. There he was an All-American basketball player. He was awarded a full basketball scholarship to Seattle Pacific University in Seattle, Washington, where he earned a B.A. degree in Business Administration. There he was the President of the Multi-Ethnic Student Association. Two years later, he earned a Master's degree in Education and a Multiple Subjects Credential from Claremont Graduate School. In addition, he earned two certificates in Spanish as a result of intensive summer course work in Ensenada, Mexico. He taught in the K-12 system for eight years, and at present, he serves as Tutorial Coordinator and instructor teaching study skills, tutor training, and English as a Second Language courses. Additionally, he is completing a second Master's degree in Instructional Technology at Cal State University San Bernardino. He will complete the degree in June 2001. He is the author of a reference book for English students entitled, ***200 Fully Conjugated English Verbs***. He is also a freelance photographer. Straight ahead!

Preface

Who is John Carlos? What makes him tick? What made him a world class sprinter, who can still sit in the stands, drinking wine, and socializing with the people? Why is he so controversial, so radical, and yet such a free spirit? And why would one of the most celebrated preachers--the prophet and social activist Dr. Martin Luther King--request to meet and speak with him about the Olympic Boycott in 1968?

Why is he so important that the FBI and the CIA investigated his every move? Why would universities across America call him to speak to their student population, knowing that he had no degree or formal training? Why do countries, to this very day, call him to come and speak about issues? Why was the demonstration that he and Tommy pulled off in Mexico such a profound statement in world history? Why does their protest symbolize an entire period of time, the 60's? These are very serious questions.

This book about John Carlos' life will answer all of these questions. John spoke openly to me about his life, and he welcomed my research and historical comments. I first met him in 1995 at College of the Desert in Palm Desert, California, where I am on the faculty as Tutorial Coordinator and instructor. Our club "African Americans for College Education" invited him to speak. As co-advisor to the club, I invited John, Eddie Joseph, a civil rights activist, and students to have lunch with me at the Sizzler Restaurant in Palm Desert. John talked to us about his life and we were fascinated by his outstanding story-telling. It was from this meeting that John and I became good friends. I visited his home on many occasions and he shared aspects of his life with me. One day I asked him if anyone was interested in writing his fascinating life story. He said that some of his friends had mentioned it, but they had never followed up on it. I asked if he would let me write it. He agreed! After purchasing a video camera, tape recorders, tapes, and other supplies, I outlined what I thought would be appropriate for a biography, and arranged to visit his home to record his story. Later, I was fortunate to meet Ms. Urla Hill, a sports historian researcher in San Jose, California. She had tons of articles, books, artifacts, and phone numbers for contacts with many of John's former teammates and coaches. She graciously shared everything with me. I did extensive research and interviews with his family members, friends, and associates from his past.

We began discussions about writing the book in 1995. It has been a delightful journey for John and me. We hope that you will find it interesting, insightful, and enjoyable. Straight Ahead!

Foreword:
On The Victory Stand

On October 16, 1968, John Carlos stood on the victory platform at the Mexico Olympics. He had placed third in the 200-meter race to win a bronze medal. Tommy Smith, an American, and Peter Norman, an Australian, winning the gold and silver respectively, stood there with him. There were 50,000 people in the stands and a billion or more observing them on television in every part of the world.

The three Olympians marched out to the stand, and the medal ceremony began. Since there were others who were to receive medals besides them, they had to wait until their places in track and field were called. Both John and Tommy put their black gloves on while they waited. When their places were called, the recipients walked up to the victory stand to receive their medals. Tommy and John had both hands behind them, carrying their running shoes. Tommy's name was called first and he received the gold medal. He walked up to the official who placed the medal over his head as he bent his 6'4" frame down to receive it. He was also given a box with an Olympic wreath in it. Standing up, he placed his running shoes on the victory stand; then he stepped up on the victory stand, raising both fists in the air due to the excitement of winning the gold medal. Peter Norman's name was called next. He walked up, kneeled, and placed himself in front of Tommy as the silver medal winner. Lastly, John's name was called. He walked up and knelt to receive the bronze medal. But before he mounted the victory stand, he placed his Puma running shoes on it. Tommy and John were standing on the victory stand in their black socks, and no one asked any questions about it. By now the black gloves that they were wearing had been detected because Tommy, forgetting in the excitement that he had a

9

glove on, had raised both hands in the air. John had stood there in the open with both hands at his side. No one in the stadium or in the world knew about the plan with the gloves, except John Carlos and Tommy Smith.

The people were cheering excitedly. The announcer for the public address system was the only thing that calmed them down. He asked that all please rise for the playing of America's National Anthem. The American flag stood tall, waving in Mexico City's thin air, and the entire stadium rose to their feet. In the meantime, Tommy, Peter, and John had to turn in another direction to face the flag. And without further ado, the playing of the National Anthem began. At the sound of the first trumpet, Tommy and John raised their fists and bowed their heads at about the same time. The majority of the people were focused on the flag, but finally it seemed that the entire stadium - the photographers, the cameras, the officials, and the other Olympians - focused their attention on the trio. Now the whole world was focused on them--standing tall, saying to America that they defied her hypocrisy, economic racism, and the way she treats people of color. As John later put it, "The American people in the stands were shocked into silence. One could hear a frog piss on cotton it was so quiet in the stadium."

Now the American People were singing in celebration of the victory in the 200-meter race. However, at the same time, in their minds, they were viewing one of the most noted, horrifying acts of defiance against American ideals. How dare they? These two black men, one from the inner-city and the other from a sharecropper's farm, who had been given the greatest opportunity to run for the greatest country in the world, at the world's most recognized and celebrated event, stand on the victory stand raising their black gloved fists in protest? You Niggers are out of place! Further, America could have chosen someone else to represent their ideals. If you had burned an American flag in Harlem or in

Fresno it would have had some repercussions, but in front of the world? This is unacceptable! America and nations around the world are here to showcase their best and you, at a most inopportune time in American History, commit a rebellious act in front of everyone. Symbolically, you two are supposed to represent your country, not put it down! You represent the fastest, strongest, and best athletes in the world. America represents truth, justice, and equality for all of its people. This is the image that the world understands about America, not this kind of insolence. America treats their Negroes well and you make the world think otherwise. This is what many of the American people were thinking as they sang that day. John said that their anger was so powerful that he could feel it coming towards him in the wind. This protest shocked the world. It reached heaven! God looked down on America that day, saying that this hour has been ordained by Him, that He has used these men as His instruments to tell the world about America's wrong against all children who should be free.

1

Beginnings

John's Birth

On June 5, 1945, around 9:27 a.m. on a rainy summer day in Harlem, New York, John Carlos was born. There were complications. Before his birth, he had often turned himself around in his mother's womb. John's mother said that the doctor would manipulate him and turn him correctly, but he would continue to turn himself around. As a result, he was a breech baby. When John was born, he already had two older brothers, Earl Jr. and Andrew; and five years later his sister Hepsey was born. The Carlos' nuclear and extended family were devoted to each other, and whenever a new child was born, all of the members would go to the hospital to see the newest addition. The baby's mother would hold the baby up in front of the window so everyone could see it.

John's parents took him home to their two-bedroom apartment at 626 Lennox Avenue in Harlem, which was filled with used furniture that was comfortable and fit the parents' taste. The most memorable piece was John's steel baby crib. The bars were an ugly silver color that reminded one of a jail cell; it was called a "jail house crib."

John was his mother's baby boy! In our interview she exuded joy with every word that she spoke about him. She laughed most of the time, and said everything that he did was an adventure. He was a short, fat, sweet boy who was adored by his parents, family, and friends. His mother said that he was spoiled, smart, extremely curious about things, and different from her other children. John developed at a much slower rate than his brothers; he did not walk until he was 2 years old. Mrs.

13

Carlos worried about his progress for a while, but in time he grew to be a powerful young man.

John says he fooled his family into believing that he could not walk by crawling when everyone was around. But, when he wanted to eat something at night, he would walk into the kitchen while his mother was away at her night shift job.

On a few occasions, he said that he would lie in his jailhouse crib, smell his mama's good Cuban cooking, climb out and sneak, undetected, into the kitchen.

> I was faster than shit on my feet, even then. I could crawl fast too. I must have been quick, if I could not have been detected walking until I turned 2 years old.

John said that his mother noticed that food was missing, and she blamed Earl Jr. or Andrew for the mess that he left after taking the food. She never suspected John because he was the baby. Earl Jr. and Andrew got spanked for John's mess, but eventually his mother found out the actual culprit.

This is how John got caught. Mrs. Carlos was cooking breakfast one morning, and John told me that his senses were aroused by the smell that caused his feet to start up like jet engines. His stomach began to growl like a hungry lion that sniffed his prey. He jumped up and climbed out of bed. He moved softly across the stiff linoleum floor and eased the door open carefully, using his peripheral vision to see if the coast was clear. It was! So he jetted out of the room. He reached his destination, the table, and he found some fried fish. The sight and smell of the fish caused his hunger to grow and he reached for a piece of it to satisfy his desire. Biting down into the fish, he saw scrambled eggs, grits, and biscuits too. So he reached into the pan, grabbed some scrambled eggs and a biscuit, gobbling some of it as he zoomed back to his room. When he arrived at his bed, he placed the remaining food through the silver bars and climbed back in to enjoy the feast. He gulped the food down hungrily. About the time he finished eating, his mother walked in to check on him. When she saw him, he had food all over his face and in the crib. She looked at him with disbelief, remembering that she had blamed Earl Jr. and Andrew for messing up her kitchen. After a while, John began to walk and run around the house, and Mrs. Carlos watched him more closely.

Another escapade got John in trouble with his mother. When he was around two or three years old, his mother had several friends and relatives visiting from Cuba. They brought her some very expensive perfumes and other items from the Islands. Mrs. Carlos was very appreciative of the gifts and she bought a beautiful tray to display the perfume bottles. She placed them in her room on her dresser. Snooping around and discovering the tray, John began to play with the bottles by an open window. Easily bored, he took the bottles and, one by one, threw them out of the window. Imagine his delight in watching those bottles drop to the sidewalk bursting into hundreds of pieces! Mrs. Carlos' response to this was: "I spank him good. I spanked him so hard that he never did anything like that again." Mrs. Carlos doesn't play!

John was very strong as an infant. Mrs. Carlos said once he was in his room playing, and he became interested in his jailhouse crib. He grabbed the guardrail, started to shake it, and after a few minutes, he decided to unhitch it. After unhitching it, he picked it up and threw it across the room, hitting the wall. It broke a hole in the wall, and the noise sounded like a New York thunderstorm. Mrs. Carlos, Earl Jr., and Andrew ran into the room, hoping that nothing serious had occurred. To their surprise, John was measuring the distance he had thrown the rail. It was difficult to believe that he had picked up and thrown that heavy jailhouse rail, and from then on, his parents and the rest of the family kept a keen eye on him.

Pop

John Carlos' father, Earl Carlos Sr., was an intelligent, well-dressed businessman and World War I Veteran. He had been born to a sharecropper in Camden, South Carolina, in 1895. Abraham Lincoln had signed the Emancipation Proclamation in 1863, just some thirty-two years before Earl Carlos was born. Earl's mother and father had been born slaves. Earl mentioned, on many occasions, how his family worked as sharecroppers, picking and chopping cotton from "can to can't." His parents fought a tough battle trying to raise eight boys and two girls. Children in the South worked at least nine months out of the year, helping their parents do the chores on the farms. And during harvesting time, it was imperative that they worked to help earn money for the family to survive. Most African-American children did not attend school, and if they did, they attended for very little time. Further, the schools were one-room buildings with only a few books, which were "seconds." Survival was the main issue for the entire family and education was secondary. Earl Sr. worked hard from an early age, yet he also understood the importance of education, of learning to read and write.

Earl came to love the "Blues," which had its beginning in Negro Spirituals. Blues--American music-was created as an expression of the feelings and emotions of African-Americans toward slavery and economic depression. It was a way to tell the white world how European-American domination affected them in all aspects of their lives. They were protest songs. Through radio airplay and 78 LP's, the "Blues" quickly became popular. W. C. Handy, the "Father of the Blues," wrote many popular songs, including: "Memphis Blues" and the world renowned "St. Louis Blues."

Ma Rainey, "Mother of the Blues," included on her shows songs entitled: "Lynch Mob Blues," "First Degree Murder Blues," "Back In Jail Blues," "No Job Blues," " Pig Meat Blues," and "Ain't Got No Money Blues." This was the type of music that Earl was exposed to in his younger days. And John can vividly recall hearing his father singing some of these songs depicting hard times for African-Americans.

The Industrial Revolution was a go. African-Americans did much of the dirty work. They were cooks, porters, waiters, shoeshine boys, newspaper boys, maids, butlers, janitors, window cleaners, and elevator men. Those who were builders and masons were considered the elite. Unfortunately, many African-Americans moved North, believing that conditions would improve, but it was the "same old game" that was being played in the South: low-paying jobs, poor housing, poor everything. Many of Earl's relatives also took part in this job migration.

Less than four years after Henry Ford made his proclamation to hire workers, Earl Carlos would face one of the most difficult times in his life: War! On April 6, 1917, under President Woodrow Wilson, the United States of America declared war on Germany. African Americans had been volunteering for active duty in the military, but one week after the declaration of war the USA refused to accept them as volunteers. On November 6, 1917, Earl was inducted into the US Army in the 371st Infantry at Camp Jackson in South Carolina. In John Hope Franklin's book entitled, *From Slavery to Freedom: A*

History of Negro Americans, he documented the actions of the 371st regiment. He stated that they arrived in France late in April in 1918. It was attached to the 157th French Division, the famous "Red Hand" under the command of General Goybet. The unit remained on the front lines for more than three months, holding first the Avocourt and later the Verrieres subsectors, northwest of Verdun. They captured a number of prisoners, machine guns, a munitions depot, railroad cars, and many other supplies. The French government decorated their regimental colors.

Earl remembered that the South resented African Americans with access to military arms training in their territory. Race riots began to break out because European-Americans were fearful that African-Americans would rebel against them because of their previous mistreatment. The riots were a show of power to keep African-Americans in line. Many were hung, castrated, tarred and feathered, raped, and shot at as a sport. The resentment escalated. To avoid more race riots, African-Americans were among the first to be sent to Europe to fight against the Germans, thus representing some of the best military soldiers the U.S. had to offer. It is ironic that they fought for the freedom of Europeans, while simultaneously being treated as second-class citizens in their homeland.

Earl Carlos and African-Americans from the South were accustomed to hard work. Many had developed strong bodies, endurance, pain tolerance, a great physique, and the idea that nothing work-wise was impossible. For some, work became a contest of strength, speed, endurance, resulting in recognition and respect. When the military inducted African-Americans into their ranks, it was similar to drafting the likes of NFL,

NBA, and other personnel from professional sporting organizations. Professor Franklin again documented the power and energy of these recruit laborers, or stevedores, needed to assist in the laborious task of providing the Allies with materials of war. One crew in France moved 1,200 tons of flour in nine and one-half hours. It was estimated that it would take several days to do the job. The French were amazed. In September 1918, a French port had 767,648 tons of goods that were mostly handled by Negroes. They moved 25,000 tons a day.

The military soldier is an athlete whose game is war. The playing field is on land, air, and sea. The soldiers use strategies, mind games, athleticism, and the human spirit to fight for freedom. It is a game of teamwork and each person has a duty to perform that may involve saving the lives of others. The African Americans who fought in the war had little time to prepare. They went to a boot camp that had the worst equipment, food, and facilities. As John's father said, they were treated 'Like Shit' by European-American soldiers, were paid less than them, and were under the direct command of white officers.

Earl told his son John that the African-Americans who fought in World War I viewed the war as a way to fight for their freedom, and they achieved great military success. The most famous group of African-Americans soldiers in World War I was the Harlem Hell Cats from the 369th Infantry in Harlem, New York. They were cited 11 times for their bravery. Citations noted the bravery and skills of these African-American soldiers who held down an entire military combat zone for two months before receiving any assistance. They were also honored for never retreating and for never being captured by the Germans. Although this was a great feat, 116,000 African-Americans soldiers died in World War I. The Harlem Hell Cats and other African-Americans played a significant role in the war through their bravery and the sacrificing of their lives.

Earl Carlos was wounded in the war--a hole in his face that remains a glaring reminder. He said that the African-Americans had two enemies, the German soldiers and some of the American officers from the South. On September 28, 1918, in the great September offense mentioned earlier under General Goybet, Earl and the "Red Hands" were in a tough battle with the Germans in Verdun. One of the white officers, having his fun, shot at Earl, hitting him in his buttocks. As Earl rose and turned towards the shooter, a German bullet pierced his left jawbone. He spent several months in a hospital in France recovering from his wounds. No military investigation of the shooting took place; Earl never revealed the truth about his first wound. He was not bitter; he was just thankful to be alive. He received the Medal of Citation Award for bravery on the battle-field.

Earl Carlos returned to the United States with new hopes and aspirations, but instead of welcoming him and his fellow black soldiers with open arms, America continued to show hatred towards blacks. Riots broke out throughout the United States because many in white America did not want to give African-Americans the economic freedom that they desired. Returning African-American soldiers hoped to claim the same first class citizenship rights they had fought and died to give Europeans during the war. Earl soon left the South to fight for economic freedom in the north. He moved to

Atlantic City, New Jersey, where some of his relatives lived, and began his quest to find economic stability. He survived the Roaring Twenties, the Stock Market Crash in 1929, the Dust Bowl in the mid-thirties, and World War II in the forties. It was during the early forties that he established a shoe repair business, one and a half blocks from Harlem's famous nightclub, the Savoy.

Earl Carlos was not only a businessman, but also a man who believed in family. In 1941, he encountered this beautiful woman in Harlem by the name of Vioris Ward. He was 24 years older than Vioris, but that did not deter him. He pursued her, captured her heart, and made her his wife.

Mama

John's mother, Louise Vioris Ward-Carlos, was born on April 20, 1919 in Jamaica. When she was one, she and her family moved to Cuba, which had been under the control of Spain until the end of the Spanish American War in 1898. Thus Mrs. Carlos' first language was Spanish; she was raised in Cuba until she was 17 years old. Her mother had died by her 10th birthday, and her Aunt, Ann Ward, raised her.

On July of 1937, her Aunt Ann summoned Vioris to America. Mrs. Ward thought that it would be easier to get her niece to the US by way of Jamaica because she was underage. So, young Vioris was placed on the Grace Line Ship from Cuba to Jamaica. After the Grace Line arrived in Jamaica, it was dry docked for two months. There Vioris remained, unable to obtain any information from the shipping office. After a while she became concerned and fearful that she was never going to leave for the US. By fate, she encountered a friend, David Solomon from Cuba. In the shipping business, he was able to contact Vioris' Aunt, and he placed the girl on board a United Fruit Line ship, which was leaving for America immediately. On December 29, 1937, Vioris Ward arrived in the US.

Vioris had two uncles, Solomon O. Ward and Luther Ward. All of the Wards were very light-skinned people. W.E.B. Dubois, an educator, writer, and activist, discusses this situation in his newspaper, *The Crisis*, where he documents the atrocities that were perpetrated on blacks. In his book, *The Souls of Black Folks*, he documented the rapes of black women in the South by white men, which produced thousands of mulatto (white and black blood) babies. These crimes were perpetrated on Cubans, Puerto Ricans, and people of other countries in the West Indies, as well as blacks. So, many of John's relatives could pass for European-Americans.

John's great-uncle, Solomon Ward, fought in World War I. He was a Lieutenant in the famous Harlem Hell Cats. John never met his Uncle Solomon who died before he was born. Nonetheless, he did get to meet Solomon's younger brother, Luther Ward. Uncle Luther was a man of great stature, standing 7' 2" tall. He looked like a European-American man with straight hair. Uncle Luther and Vioris were very close.

Vioris Carlos was a hard-working woman. She took two buses to go across town, sometimes in the cold bitter winters, to clean European-American houses to supplement Earl's income. She spent long hours scrubbing floors and bathroom tiles. Everything was done by hand during those days, and the work was extremely hard on her back, hands and knees. She not only cleaned for a living, but she cleaned and cooked at home, too. John doesn't know where she got the strength, but he thinks they call it love.

One day, Mrs. Carlos got tired of cleaning, and she enrolled in a trade school. She earned a certificate to become a nurse's aide. After completing the program, she worked at Bellevue Hospital for fifteen years. While working for the hospital, she continued to travel by bus, working a graveyard shift from 12:00 p.m. to 8:00 a.m. five days a week. With both parents working, the Carlos family was more financially stable than others were.

Harlem

"When I die," John Carlos told me, "my last wish will be to have my body burned, my ashes flown in a helicopter or plane and poured out over the city that I love, Harlem. It will be a permanent place of rest for my body until God comes."

He says that Harlem is his heart and soul. In the 20's it saw the rebirth of African American culture in a three-and-a-half square mile of land on Manhattan Island, a magnet that attracted the most talented intellectuals, artists, writers, playwrights, activists, athletes, social scientists, and musicians from every part of American society and the world. John was well acquainted with Harlem's magnanimity, and he feels strongly about sharing the experiences of two generations of Carlos who watched Harlem develop into a great culturally rich city.

John's father, Earl Carlos Sr., came from the generation of the 1920's that witnessed the Harlem Renaissance Period. He saw many churches spring up, with preachers like Adam Clayton Powell Sr. and Adam Clayton Powell Jr. of the Abyssinian Baptist Church. Their preaching caused masses of people to come together to form a new religious and political alliance. From this amalgamation, the eighteenth district was established, and Harlem sent a representative to the US Congress in 1944. Congressman Adam Clayton Jr. became Harlem's new representative. Everybody in Harlem knew of him and they were proud to have Congressman Powell represent them. John's father also spoke of the legacy of Father Divine, the man who set up soup kitchens during the Great Depression in the thirties, giving African-

Americans hope by teaching them to be self-reliant and moral.

John's father was a high-ranking member in the Elks Lodge. This Secret Society, like the Masons, Rosicrucians, Knights of Columbus, and the Eastern Star for the women, gave prominence to members who upheld their secrets. Presidents, judges, governors, senators, policemen, preachers, and top officials around the world were members. The secret societies in the Western World obtained their knowledge from the tombs of the black African kings, queens, and priest scientists in Egypt. This is an important point because many people believe the Eurocentristic fallacies, promoted in American history, that the ideas of the Western world are indigenous to Europe. Earl Carlos was well known in the community, thus allowing him to associate with two of the oldest black organizations in the country, the NAACP and the Urban League. W.E.B. Dubois and James Weldon Johnson were the two pioneers that established these organizations and relocated their main offices in Harlem.

John remembers that the people in Harlem were very proud to have their own newspapers. He and his cronies established a hustle on the streets selling <u>Jet</u> and <u>Ebony</u> magazines. He was too young to know anything about the <u>New York Amsterdam</u> and the <u>New York Age Newspaper</u>, but his mom and dad can recall hearing the newspaper boys shouting, "Extra, extra, read all about it, get it while it's hot cause Harlem's news got news." Marcus Garvey, one of John's favorite heroes, brought his organization, the Universal Negro Improvement Association, to Harlem, thus creating a great impact on the people of the city. The Association called on Negroes to think about returning to Africa. John recalls the parades celebrating the legacy of Mr. Garvey, one of the first black men who influenced Harlem.

John's description of Harlem's day and night life was exciting! It was impossible to be bored; the place was alive, hot, and jumping. The Apollo Theater, where some of the greatest singers, dancers, comedians, and singing groups performed. Even today, many entertainers get their start on its stage.

John gives no other individual the kind of recognition that he bestows upon the late great Paul Robeson. Paul was held in high esteem due to his multifaceted career: an actor and singer in Shakespearean plays and American television; a scholar and all-American athlete at Rutgers University; the ability to speak over 8 languages; and an activist for truth and equality. To John, Paul Robeson symbolizes what a man should be.

Earl described the Cotton Club as the best-known club in Harlem. Duke Ellington, Cab Calloway, Lena Horn, and others of the greatest performers in American history, starred there. Unfortunately African-Americans could not patronize the club because wealthy European-Americans (whites) and the mob hung out there. Nonetheless, African-Americans could view the performances of the artists in other clubs and dance halls.

John's favorite entertainment place was the Savoy Ballroom, the Home of the Happy Feet, which presented the Big Bands like Count Basie, Lionel Hampton and others. His father owned and operated a shoe repair place a half block away from it. In fact, Mr. and Mrs. Carlos knew Duke Ellington, Lena Horn, Count Basie, Dinah Washington, and many other stars personally. Many of these stars from the Savoy patronized their shoe shop for shoe repairs, shoeshines, cigarettes, and other goods. John's mother spoke lovingly and enthusiastically about the times that she and her husband would lie in bed and listen to the beautiful music flow from the Savoy. Although John was not old enough to see the shows, he earned a large sum opening cab doors for the Savoy's rich clients.

On every street corner in the downtown section, one could see and hear the skit and the skat of feet-tapping rhythms of the times. Adults and children alike tried to imitate the tappers because it was the thing to do. But the one name that stands out is the King of Tap, the legendary William "Bojangles" Robinson, also nicknamed "The Mayor of Harlem."

John mentioned many inspiring people: poet Langston Hughes; novelist James Baldwin; actor Paul Robeson; photographer Gordon Parks; superstar athletes Jackie Robinson, Goose Tatum, Wilma Rudolph and Sugar Ray Robinson; artist James Vanderzee; and social scientist and philosopher Alain Locke. But the person who was the most influential was his father, Earl Carlos Sr.

Many of these cultural icons crossed John's path on the streets of Harlem, in its theaters, on the radio and TV, and in conversations with the people who lived there. He was grateful to have been exposed to their talents while growing up in Harlem.

2

Grade School Days

Ringworm

The first day of school was a disaster for John. Somehow, before school began, he caught ringworm, which appeared as scales on his head. John's mother Vioris used a woman's stocking and a sailor's cap to cover his head. He pleaded with his mother not to send him to school because of his embarrassment. His mother understood how he felt and told him that if he attended school, he did not have to take his hat off in class.

Although John's mother had assured him that he could leave his hat on, he still worried about the consequences, since it was considered proper etiquette for males to remove their hats inside buildings. When he arrived at school, his mother took him to the office to be enrolled. Even in this strange, new environment, all he could focus on was the gear upon his head. As he walked towards his new classroom, he felt anxious, nervous and excited. Mrs. Carlos and John walked into the classroom where other children mingled. The teacher, a long-legged brunette, introduced herself, and John's mother left. The school bell rang and the students were instructed to sit in assigned seats. The teacher began roll call and when she called his name, she looked up at him and politely asked him to remove his hat. Her request filled John with anxiety; he wanted two things, his mother and a quick exit from that room. He felt trapped, and the result was his terse reply indicating his mother's permission to leave the hat on. John recalled, "I felt as if my heart had fallen through my body and had crashed to the floor."

Cleavy Davis, a "smart ass" kid, thought that he would solve the problem by running and snatching both the stocking cap and hat off John's head from behind.

This action caused something to snap inside John, and he told me he immediately wanted "to kick some ass." Both boys fought like two wild animals, throwing chairs, tables and books at each other. The other students were screaming with excitement until the teacher broke up the fight. John was so angry that he cried continuously. When the school officials called his mother - who returned and explained the reason for the headgear - the teacher, now understanding John's stubbornness, allowed him to return to class. Eventually, John and Cleavy made up and became close.

Hustling

John learned to work at a very early age. Every day after school, he was required to work in the family's shoe repair business, cleaning and shining shoes and stocking the goods. He did not like doing those tasks, and was bold enough to tell his parents. But out of respect for his parents, John did his chores without an attitude.

John always hustled his own money. After he finished his chores, he and his brother Andrew would work in front of the popular Savoy Ballroom, which stayed open 24 hours a day. Most of the clients that patronized the Savoy arrived by cab, and as the cab drivers dropped them off, Andrew and John would open the doors for tips. Some of the women clients gave John extra large tips due to his good looks. Andrew also earned good money because the Savoy clients were very generous.

John saved his money, accruing as much as $2000. From earning the money and saving it, he learned the value of a dollar. On occasion, Earl Carlos, swallowing his pride, borrowed money from his son. John was thankful that his father felt comfortable enough to ask for money, but not so prideful that he was risking his manhood. Of course, it was ironic that Earl Carlos had to borrow money in that he owned his own business. Nonetheless, John continued to use his light-skinned good looks and a charming personality to earn money.

During this time, John, his brothers, and a few friends created the "Harlem Side Show" to earn money by playing off John's light-skinned good looks and winning personality. The ambitious young men made musical instruments, congas, and drums, from leftover materials found in ice cream and coconut factories. They then rehearsed with the finished instruments with John as the dancing star of the show.

John said, "I danced! I wasn't shy at all! I would shake my little ass up and down and all around. We got paid!" The people from the streets and the Savoy loved to watch the show and would fill their hats with tips. Sometimes, pretty ladies would pick John up, kiss him, and give him a special tip. The group was a success, and they were able to earn some serious money. John and his brothers had a curfew of 6 p.m., so they had to take care of business during the day. The three Carlos brothers had plenty of cash to spend, and the neighborhood kids would gather under their apartment window to take turns doing candy runs. The money was tied to a string and lowered to the waiting "runners" who used the cash to buy candy. All then equally shared the candy.

John said many positive things about the parents of his neighborhood. Every adult was a surrogate parent, and they took an interest in what their children did. So a child had to be very careful about their conduct, because if you screwed up, it got back to your parents. When you got home, you got your ass beat on top of the one you may have gotten out there in the streets. The parents of his day did not play!

The Prophetic Vision

John's father took them to church every Sunday ever since they were four and five years old. He was a devout Catholic who gave his tithes to the church by providing free shoe repair for the Father and some of the Nuns of his parish. John remembered how his father did his Hail Mary, how the Father's robe and the Nuns' head-draped uniforms looked.

John said that he remembered nothing spiritual about church and prayer until he reached the age of seven. He had a spiritual vision!

I do recall having a vision of an event like the one in Mexico City. This is a recollection of how the Lord revealed the event to me. This experience was unlike a dream. I was awake! The vision began like this. I was lying down in my room alone in a relaxed state resting -- just allowing my mind to wander like a normal child would do. I looked up, and all of a sudden, I began to feel myself moving up and outside of my body. This was not an out of body experience, but it seemed like one. I felt at peace, not feeling or experiencing any fear. I was not aware of the time frame, but all at once, I saw what appeared to be a large screen. I looked into the screen and a picture appeared to me. The experience was like turning on a big screen TV. The picture came into focus instantly, and I saw thousands of people sitting in a large arena. And as quickly as I saw the people in the stands, it was as if the vision focused a direct shot on me. I was looking at myself standing on a platform. I heard the voices of the people in the stands, and the focus of their attention was upon me. The voices turned into cheers, and the thousands of hands that waved looked like branches from trees. Everyone was cheering for me! The atmosphere was high-spirited. The sun shone bright, and I became excited! I said to myself that this was the coolest thing that I have ever seen! My ego shot high, and I said to myself that I must be something special! I don't know what it is that I'm going to do, but I'm the man! These people are honoring me! Hey, I know! I am going to be rich and famous! All kinds of good things went through my mind. I was sitting on top of the world! Then suddenly, something tragic happened! I don't know what it was, but just as quickly as the people were praising me and cheering me, they began to boo me. The vision subsided, the screen closed and I came back into myself.

I held on to the positive part of the vision, because the Lord did not show me the reason for the sudden booing. So that evening, I told my mother, father, sister, and brothers about the vision. I was excited! I mean, I really knew from that point in my life that I was going to be rich and famous. I tried my best to explain the vision that I had, but as a seven-year-old child, I could not articulate very well. After I explained my vision to my family, they looked at me and

said, "Okay." Two things happened to me after
that vision. The first thing that I noticed was a
void in my life. From that point on, I looked for
religion. I began to ask questions about God
and why things were the way they were in this
world. Secondly, I began to tell my brothers
and sister that I was going to be famous and
rich one day. Nonetheless, my family is a
witness to the fact that I had this vision, and
later on in life, all of us would find out it's
meaning.

John's older brother Earl Jr. clearly recalled the
story about the vision:

The people may not believe it, but it is true.
John told all of the immediate family that he
had had a dream and it was real to him. He told
us that he was going to be rich and famous
based on a dream where he had seen people in
a stadium cheering him on.

The story about the prophetic vision was fascinating;
from that point he knew that he was destined to do
something great.

TV

Television raised many questions in John's mind. It was a rare commodity in his neighborhood. His family was one of the first families in Harlem to own one. Before television, every family listened to the radio. John had several programs that he listened to on a weekly basis. "Johnny Dollar," a detective story, was his favorite program, but when TV came, he became hooked on it. He could see the characters with his eyes and did not need to depend on his imagination. After watching TV for a while, John had a major concern. He noticed that something was missing. He said that after watching all of the various programs he realized that none of them had blacks walking or driving down the streets, sitting in restaurants, coming out of stores, or doing anything that one does in society. He only saw black actors and actresses playing butlers, maids, and cooks. This was not acceptable to John, and he began to ask questions as to why blacks did not have parts as characters in mainstream society in Hollywood films. His parents wondered how he could be so perceptive in noticing roles for black actors. John lived in a time when blacks had been very successful in breaking down some of the walls of oppression. He saw many positive role models--congressmen, preachers, teachers, activists, musicians, athletes, writers, Master Masons, and businessmen in his own community. Knowledge is ageless!

John was never the typical kind of person who accepted everything as right and true. He questioned everything! He absorbed the information that was around him. His listening began at home with his father, and when he got big enough to work in the shoe shop, he listened to customers (from the average person to famous people) talk about the conditions that Negroes faced in this country. This kind of interaction went on in barber shops, on Harlem street corners, in beauty shops, in churches, in clubs, in parks, in Gospel songs, in Blues and Jazz music, in Negro paintings and pictures, in Negro books, in theaters and dance, in Goose Tatum moves on playgrounds, in white folks' kitchens, with jobless youth, with mothers on buses, with fatherless children, with fathers with no job or education, on rooftops, and in the white man's subconscious. In Harlem, one is exposed to everything that is done under the sun.

John asked his teachers the same questions that he asked his parents about Negroes not being on mainstream TV. None of them could give him a clear answer. In fact, their attitude was that he shouldn't be asking them questions like that. But he felt he had every right to ask those questions. As a matter of fact, all of Harlem had a right to ask these questions, but the masses were uneducated and simply struggling to survive. John said that this was one of the first things that turned him off from wanting to learn in school. Further, he noticed that throughout history, in the Bible, and in anything that was important, white people accomplished everything.

'What did Negro people do in history?' I never hear about Negroes doing anything. I told them that had it not been for the Jr. High School in my neighborhood, named after a Negro by the name of Frederick Douglas, I wouldn't know that we did anything. I knew that my father had fought in World War I, and I asked why we didn't discuss that.

He was so vocal that he got the interest of the other students. He had created a following, and this was not acceptable to the teachers and administrators. They immediately labeled him a troublemaker. The principal called his parents to school and asked them questions about his motives to encourage other students to protest the fact that there was no Negro heroes being taught in the curriculum. John's parents stood up for him, and they felt that he was right. The authorities were disappointed with his parents' response, and John continued to protest. The situation got worse, and they could not contain him. Eventually, he was suspended from school because of his ability to influence other black students to see that they were not being given a fair education.

Heroes

John has always had heroes in his life. His first and foremost hero was his dad. He understood what it meant to have someone to look up to when it came to learning about things in life:

In order to teach a child properly in education, it is imperative that he learns about his group's contribution in history. One needs to see someone who looks like him in order to identify with self. In school, blacks had no heroes. Personally, I had several of them, namely my father, Earl Carlos, Paul Robeson, Frederick Douglas, Adam Clayton Powell (I attended his church), John Brown, Bill Robinson, and many others. We never discussed them in school, and it was forbidden to do so at the time. Nonetheless, the white children saw images that looked like them all the time. Jesus, angels, presidents, governors, mayors, senators, judges, the media, billboards, materials in textbooks, and every phase of society represented people who looked white. One can't miss feeling proud, self-reliant, intelligent, and beautiful after seeing people who have done the important things in society look like him.

The authorities knew this! The school curriculum was designed with white superiority in mind. And by keeping the truth suppressed about the blacks' contributions in mathematics, science, ancient astrology, architecture, medicine, theology, health, nutrition, and other related subjects, the authorities could systematically keep us disinterested in school. One must be able to identify with self in order to learn. I understood this concept early, and I was crucified by the authorities for sharing the truth with my fellow students. And just like the system is designed to do, my friends and I were turned off, because we could not identify with the white teachers or the characters in the curriculum that did not look like us.

I did just enough work to appease the teachers in order to graduate. But the main thing that I wanted the teachers and the administration to know was that I was not going to allow them to teach me without teaching me something about the black contributions. I made them respond to me, and I made them think about their actions when it came to teaching the truth. I made them respect me, and I reminded them that every black student was not dumb enough to believe the hypocrisy and lies that they were teaching us in school. They may have labeled me a troublemaker, but deep down in their psyche, I caused them to think about our situation as blacks.

Think about this for a moment. The teachers were teaching us that George Washington was always honest, and he proved his honesty by telling his parents that he chopped down a cherry tree. I know for a fact that my grandparents on my father's side of the family were slaves.

41

President Washington was a slave owner. I knew the terrible conditions that the slaves had to endure, because we as a people are still going through hard economic times. My question is was I supposed to be happy about George Washington's honesty, knowing that he had the power as President to help correct the immoral acts of slavery in this country, and he did nothing? Heavens no! Explaining to the teachers that the Negro is somebody makes me proud of what I did in grade school.

I noticed other serious issues in the parochial school that I attended. I noticed that the white teachers' would treat the students as if they didn't care. And when a student would raise their hand to ask a question or say that they could not see the board the teacher's response was, 'Oh, you can't see the board. Are you blind?' It wasn't that the kid was blind, the kid simply needed glasses, and his family could not afford to buy them. Further, the teacher would demand that the student come to the board, and upon arriving, the teacher would rub their nose against it and say, 'Can you see it now?' This was a tactic that one teacher would use to keep students in line and avoid the problem altogether. Eventually I was kicked out of Catholic school.

My parents enrolled me into public school that fourth grade year. I found refuge in a teacher named Mrs. Seneca. She was a Negro woman who could pass for white. She took a great interest in me, and she made great efforts in trying to increase my deficient reading skills.

Her efforts were useless! For at that particular time, I now know that I had dyslexia. Dyslexia is a disturbance of the ability to read. During that era, the schools didn't have a name for my problem. The teachers called the students who had it 'stupid.'

The school officials' assessment of me never deterred me from believing that I was nothing less than brilliant. I discerned this fact because I was in a situation where I was misunderstood by a white society who misrepresented the African American.

I knew that I was different because I could not read and write like other students. Consequently, I began to drift away from reading activities. Further, I recall some of the cruel tactics that the teachers used to handle students like myself with similar problems. Out of all the ones that I can recall, the most humiliating was the "dunce corner." The dunce corner was a place where a student had to sit for hours with a cone hat on their head. To me, this was uncalled for, and I did not want to go and sit in a corner because I could not read. Thus, I became the class clown! I did everything in my power to get myself out of being chosen to read. And you know what? The clowning around kept me from reading, and at the same time, it turned into a nightmare, because the school officials referred me and others to see a psychologist. I guess they felt that I was crazy.

The last two years of elementary was a roller coaster ride for me. I continued to challenge the teachers, and they continued to shift me back and forth to the principal and the school psychologist. I had created a bad reputation with the teachers, and many of them knew me by name.

The Carlos Name

The last name "Carlos" has caused many people to wonder what John's ethnic background is. His last name was never a question for him until one day some weird name-calling started in the fourth grade. John was strolling across campus, handling things as he normally did, and out of the clear blue, this kid called him a strange name. He asked the kid what the hell he was talking about, because he had not heard anything like it before. So the kid explained to John that his last name was foreign, and Negroes did not have that kind of name. So, since he had the last name Carlos, John could not be a Negro. He said that he had to be something else. Further, he said that he was not an American. He said that he must be from some other place, and he wanted John to know what the name he called meant. John said that under normal circumstances, he would "kick a dude's ass" about calling him out of his name, but this was different. This kid went to the root and John was forced to find out his identity. John said that the kid's explanation about his name threw him off guard, and he didn't know how to respond. So, he gave him the brush off and spared him an "ass whuuping," due to the seriousness of the matter. "That kid really messed with my mind," he said, and he began to wonder about his last name. He began to think, "I know that my mother was born in Jamaica, and my father was born in South Carolina." All kinds of things ran through his mind, and he couldn't wait to get home from school that day. He desperately needed to talk to his father about his last name.

Earl Sr. came in from the shop around six-thirty, and the family would come to the kitchen to have supper. Supper was a time for conversation, and Earl Sr. usually controlled the topics of discussion. The conversation could stem from their general activities to what was happening in the news. He always seemed to have a good grasp of what was going on. That night after supper John approached his father, and asked him about the Carlos name. He explained to his father that what the kid from school had said bothered him. John's father, moved, began to explain in vivid detail the history of the Carlos name:

Son, before the white man discovered America, our forefathers lived in West Africa. We were a proud people having our own language, culture, religion, music, college, universities, schools, governments, and massive amounts of gold and precious metals. The Europeans discovered this knowledge and wealth during the time they were exploring the world. So, they needed laborers to do their work, and that is where we fit into the equation.

The African kings, along with the European slave traders, took and bought many Africans to America for slave labor. The name 'Carlos' went through a slight change during the transition from Africa to America. The name 'Carlos' was originally 'Carlo.' I was told by my father that the name was changed in Spain after his relatives escaped off the ship when it docked in Spain. Adding an "s" to Carlo gave it a Spanish form. Those who had escaped were eventually captured, and they were taken to South Carolina. Today, we have many relatives who live in that area. So, Son, that is how you got the last name Carlos. Don't you ever forget what I told you, and always be proud of who you are. You are just as much American as any white or black man in this country. As I have mentioned before, Son, myself and others have fought or died to make this country as great as it is. So hold your head up high, and know that you are somebody.

When Earl Sr. told John that story he felt good inside. Now he had a history and a name that he could be proud of. John moved through the school system lacking the necessary skills to become a successful student. He graduated from elementary school with the lowest mark and a confidential file that was sent to his teachers in junior high school.

3

Jr. High School Days

Frederick Douglas Jr. High

John attended Frederick Douglas Jr. High School in Harlem. Douglas had large four-story buildings that housed at least 8,000 students. The bell system caused a mass migration from one class to another. John found that the students were much larger in stature than those who attended his elementary school. Douglas was like a city in its own right, and one had to know how to survive. It was a wake up call for John and his homies.

At Douglas, self-preservation was the law. Jr. High School was a different world with different elements. One had to learn to protect oneself due to the violence that took place on the campus. Students brought in various weapons and it was imperative that one learned to protect oneself from thugs, thieves, and bullies. It was important to know who these individuals were. John said that school was school, but it was not a school for the purpose of learning. It was a place where students gathered to learn about social contact. It is the same concept that occurs in prison where inmates teach each other their crafts. Students learn hands-on how to be criminals. John had already been out there on the streets hustling and learning about life in the real world, and around that time, he was experimenting with sex, drugs, and the numbers game. He also wanted to know what it was like to be a gangster.

John has always considered himself a lover. When he was about ten years old, there was a girl named Ruth Ann who lived upstairs from him. She turned John on to the sex thing. She would invite him into her room and get freaky with him. She taught him different ways

49

to get her off. She also taught John how little boys get off too. It was from that point on that he was turned on to sex. After he reached puberty, he said that his light skin, height, strong posture, and handsome face caught the attention of the older ladies. Ruth Ann had already taught him the sex thing, and he let the women know that he knew what was going on.

He gave me an example of what he was talking about by mentioning that he was a good friend of the late, great songstress Dinah Washington's son. He said that on many occasions he visited her son to hang out. He gave details about how Dinah used to play her records as she did her household chores. Dinah was a very beautiful woman, and men were vying for her hand all of the time. However, quiet as it has been kept, John said that Dinah had somehow allowed John to know that she had an interest in him. It would be a situation where a mature woman like Dinah could take a young guy like John and mold him into what she wanted in a man. John had other women like Dinah who had some interest in him, but he was moving so fast that they didn't know when they would see him from one day to the next. From moving fast, he started drinking wine and smoking marijuana. He got loaded all the time with his homies. John said that the Gallo Company should have paid him a bonus for all the wine that he and his homies purchased in Harlem.

Alcohol and tobacco companies have targeted poor black communities like Harlem for many years. Harlem had a liquor store on every corner, and on top of that, the billboards advertised to everyone that it was cool to drink and smoke. At the same time, drugs were being trafficked into the community as well. John knew about heroin because he knew many users. He stumbled on to cocaine by accident. John used to work for his Aunt Lina cleaning houses and abortion clinics. Abortions were illegal, but doctors were performing them on a daily basis. So when his Aunt Lina took him to help her clean these clinics, John would snoop around the doctors' desks to see what he could find. On several occasions, he discovered cocaine. He did not know what it was then; however he used to take the powder and rub it on his gums. The numbness gave him a different feeling, and he took some home with him each time he found it.

John was a natural born fighter! At Douglas and on the streets, he had begun to establish a reputation for his fighting skills. He was not a bully. He fought to protect family, friends, and people in trouble. A rebel, warrior, and leader who fought for what he thought was right, he didn't "take shit" from anyone. As he described some of the things that he fought against, the scene would come to life before your eyes. When he came to a part that was dramatic, he spoke as if it were happening now. His voice would become strong, unsmiling, and he'd let you know that the situation was serious then and still serious now!

On several occasions, we [meaning blacks] had to fight whites just to go to the movies in the Bronx. I thought about the things that my father had been telling me about the fact that he had put his life on the line to defend the rights, liberties, and the pursuit of happiness for the citizens of this country, and when people in Harlem had to fight to get a job, fight to have a place to live, or fight just to go to another part of town, this really got me disturbed. Blacks fought and died for this country, and the Carlos family made a contribution towards the cause. Now when I say things like this, no one wants to hear that shit. Blacks are just supposed to keep quiet and take other people's shit. Not John Carlos! So when I encountered an individual who felt that I had no right to go and come as a citizen, I went dead off on his ass!

One day I got into a confrontation with some whites about coming in on what they said was their turf. The turf that they were speaking of was a public place in the Bronx, and that was the movie theater. They did not like the blacks coming over into their area, and I told them that I was going to come over there, whether they like it or not, because I was ready to kick anyone's ass that tried to stop me from coming. I got into it with one of them, and I beat him down. I knocked him out cold! After the knock out, I took my dick out and I pissed all over him, and I told his homies saying, "When he wakes up, tell him that John Carlos pissed in his face and I will be back again." And I continued by saying, "Tell him that if he is a man, he will come looking for me." The whites and my homies thought that I was crazy. I wasn't crazy. I just wanted to let them know that I meant business, and I didn't care about life or death when it came down to the cause. As a matter of fact, not too many people would have taken the situation as far as I did. They would probably have kicked the dude's ass and left. Not me! I wanted to leave an everlasting impression in his mind. So if I died, I wanted them to think that there were many more crazies like me ready to get off in someone's ass when they got out of line. I was ready to do battle with anyone who challenged my freedom. I was a rebel from the past because I had not seen too many people during that time who would fight so hard to make a statement that we were not going to take any shit without a fight. I believe that during the 1900's through the 1920's we had more fighters like myself. I am not saying that I was the only one ready to fight; I am saying that I had not run into very many people like myself.

He had a different agenda from the rest because he understood the times better than most.

John ran the numbers while attending Douglas, too. The horses, you know! He used to hang out with the senior bookies. He was important to them because they could use him to carry numbers when the Irish cops tried to shake them down. In those days, the cops never expected a young, good-looking kid like John would carry them. John was adamant about stating that many cops were crooked, not caring what any person did as long as they got a cut. The shakedown took place because the numbers runners did not give the cops a cut to allow them to operate. John said, "Blacks earned lots of money on the numbers, and the whites did not like it because blacks were not selling their dope to earn the money. Many in America were betting on horses, and the whites had to find a way to control it. So they created off-track betting. This knocked-off revenues from those who had that hustle, and they had to find a way to earn a living in other areas. The job market was run by whites, and education was closed to blacks. So many blacks resorted to selling drugs or heroin for the whites to earn money. All of this was going on during my Junior High School days, and I learned to be a leader in the halls of the four-story buildings. I had already lost interest in the school system, and I was absorbing everything that took place outside of the classroom."

John stated that some teachers at Douglas were wild and treacherous too. They would get off in a student's ass very quick using their hands, paddles, and whatever else was necessary to get their point across. He told me about a muscle-bound teacher with an attitude who kicked the ass of one of his homies named James (Log Head) for being in the wrong part of the building. James told John what had happened, and John told him that he and the rest of the group were planning to kick the teacher's ass.

John had five guys whose names were Dorian, Raymond, Cleavy, Harry, and Alvin who hung out with him through thick and thin. He called them together, and told them about the incident. John explained that the teacher was going to pay for what he had done. John's father had told him about using his head before his anger and emotion got the best of him. He told him that it is better to get in a man's pocket by using the authorities than to beat him down. John wanted to get into the teacher's pocket by using his own methods, so he and his homies got information about the kind of car that the teacher owned. They set up a time when they felt it was safe to do damage to it. So when the time was right, this is what they did: They broke out all of the windows on the teacher's sports car, and then they turned it over on its side. John had purchased some gasoline, and he poured it on the car. He then took a match, struck it, and set the car on fire. After he set it on fire, they ran to a secret place, where they rejoiced about what they had done.

The authorities never discovered who torched the car, and John took the incident further. A few days later, he went to a cop on the street, and he asked him what would happen if an adult beat a student--putting marks on his body. The cop told him that it was not legal, and the adult was in violation of child abuse laws. So, he told the cop that a teacher at school had beaten one of his friends. The cop was alarmed, and he told John to meet him at school the next day. He also indicated that it was important for all involved to bring their parents. Thanking the cop, John told James what to do. The next morning, the cop came to school, and each one of the students brought his parents with him. James told the principal what had happened, and the teacher was called into the office. When he walked in, he was surprised to see everyone there. When he looked at James, he didn't smile, and he knew that he had messed up. So the principal explained the situation to the teacher, and without any hesitation, the teacher confessed. The room got quiet, and the principal indicated that certain disciplinary action would take place, and neither John nor Douglas Junior High School saw that teacher again.

John described Douglas as a place where anything could happen:

WHY? The Biography of John Carlos

Man, the shit that these kids are experienceing today ain't nothing new. Shit, I can remember walking into the restroom to take a piss, and I did the normal thing that a dude would do when he goes into the restroom. When I walked through the door I check in all directions as to what is going on in the immediate environment. It was when I looked up that startled the shit out of me. I looked up, and I saw a guy hanging from his neck, deader than a motherfucker! I stood back in horror--looking around to see if anyone else was around to see how they were responding. No one else was around! So I forgot all about taking a piss, and I got my ass out of there. I said to myself, "What the hell was that all about, and who in the hell did that to homeboy!" So, I was used to a hostile environment, and I let the people know that Johnny did not take any shit, no matter what the state of mind the other individuals might be in. If anything, I might be just as crazy or crazier than any one of them.

Survival was the name of the game, and one had to establish himself in order to be left alone.

Although John was learning many wrong things from being in the fast lane, he had developed a real concern about the living conditions of the students who attended his school. He wanted to know who had things and who didn't. Therefore, he began to investigate individuals who got a free lunch, those who had enough money to live in an apartment without the assistance of other families, and those who had enough money to buy heating during the winter, etc. And during his investigation, he found out that many of the students came to school hungry; others couldn't afford to buy heating during the winter; and basically, the majority of people who attended his school were poor and hungry.

Robin Hood

The television and movie industry are the most powerful mediums in the world. They have been used to spread propaganda, influence people to buy goods and services, and to brainwash people into thinking or believing certain ideas, concepts, and philosophies about society and the people who live in them. The movie "Robin Hood" had a very powerful impact on John. He had been experimenting with sex, drugs, alcohol, the numbers, and gangsterism. But at the same time, he was socially conscious about the way others lived and why. He had discovered that the majority of the students that attended Douglas were poverty stricken. When John saw the movie "Robin Hood" he was able to identify with it completely. He understood the oppression King John placed on the people by overtaxing them -- collecting money and crops. The same thing was happening in Harlem, with business and government controlling the money, jobs and real estate, and collecting taxes. The Sheriff of Nottingham was the tax collector. The Irish cops were John's Sheriff of Nottingham. They did not collect taxes, but they patrolled the streets, keeping blacks from moving about in the white parts of town. John's perception of the movie, relating it to his own environment, demonstrates his ability to understand language in stories and the powerful messages presented.

Robin Hood, a white man in green tights, who stole from the rich and gave to the poor, was someone John could identify with. He was so excited after seeing the movie that he went and saw it again several times. Each time it sparked ideas in his head as to how he could devise a plan to emulate his fictional movie hero Robin Hood. After a while, the idea of becoming Harlem's Robin Hood became an obsession with him.

The housing in Harlem had become old and dilapidated. Most of the homes and apartments were thirty or more years old, and it was time to renovate or build new homes and apartments. So John and his family had to move from Lennox Avenue. They moved to one block from Yankee Stadium. The city of New York was in the process of building project homes in many places. The first projects to be built in Harlem were the Harlem River Projects, where at least one fifth of the people in Harlem would wind up living.

Yankee Stadium was built near the Harlem River and the railroad yard. The ships would come in to load and unload products and goods to be delivered to market by train. John had been spying on the operation for months, and he noticed that at certain times during the day the workers left the railroad yards unattended. John brought this to the attention of his friends, and they watched the scene with him. They watched for a week or two, and John decided to have a meeting to discuss the details about what they were going to do to obtain the goods. Everyone in the group saw John as their leader, and John knew that his friends' motives were to steal the goods to earn some money. But John had other ideas. On the day of the meeting, they were sitting and looking at the railroad yard. John had become familiar with some of his friends' ideas as they observed the activities of the men who worked in the railroad yard.

I demanded the group's attention by saying, "Listen up everyone. I have been observing the railroad yard for quite some time, and you have observed it for the last couple of weeks. I know that some of you are interested in getting the goods in order to sell them to earn some money. This is not my motive for breaking and entering. My motive is to get the goods and share them with all of the poor families in our community. I have been thinking deeply about how many of the students at Douglas don't have enough money to buy food and heating during the winter. I was shocked to find out that most of them did not have a damn thing to eat. I also know that some of you can use some extra food in your homes, and you know some people who live near you who need it, too. All of you know that we sell blood to the hospital when we ditch school in order to get money to go to the movies."

Some of their heads began to nod, while others looked on, agreeing with their eyes. So I said to them, "Do you remember 'Robin Hood'?" They said, "Yes, man that movie was damn good." Then I explained to them that I had been thinking about what Robin Hood did in the movie to help his people to eat/survive. I explained to them that we had a great opportunity to do the same thing by breaking into the trains and taking the food to the hungry people in Harlem. I explained to them that it was not about the money; it was about helping others. I told them that I was very serious about taking on this operation, and I wanted to know if they were down with me.

Every one of my friends got fired up at what I had said to them, and all of them responded by saying, "I'm down with you, Johnny." I was so happy that they did not go against the idea that we were not going to steal to earn money, but it would be to help others. In concluding, I told them that once we take care of the people in need, and if we had some goods left, we would sell them only to those who could afford it.

John, and about six of his friends, began hitting the trains the very next day. The only tool that they needed was a hammer (to break the locks on the train doors). Sometimes they didn't need anything at all because the trains would use a seal on the doors. This made the burglary even easier for them. Each member in the group had to be strong, fast, and in excellent condition because they had to carry twenty-five pound boxes, while running two to three miles across the 155th Street Bridge. All of this activity was done during the early evening, when the sun was shining bright.

The burglaries went on for about three months, and they got real good at their craft. They got so good that they built carts out of wood and roller-skates. It was during this time that many hungry people in Harlem ate like kings and queens. The trains were filled with fruits, vegetables, meats of all kinds, poultry, lamb, and fish. They even had Succotash! The boxes upon boxes they brought to the poor families brought smiles to many a hungry face. John said that it made him feel good inside to see the people have something extra to eat, and the kids could go to school without being hungry. He also said that his friends were happy about the situation.

Further, after distributing food to everyone, they had the opportunity to sell the extra food.

Although John and his friends had a one hundred percent success rate, there came a time when they almost were caught. The train workers noticed that many of their freight cars had been vandalized, and they reported it to the police. So, the police and the train people set up a trap. They found out that John and his crew were from Harlem, and they had to carry the goods across the 155th Street Bridge when it opened its gates to allow traffic and ships to pass to bring the goods to their destination. The plan was to call the bridge operator and have him close the bridge before the bandits could pass. Then, John and his crew would have nowhere to go, and without a doubt, the police would catch them. John thought ahead, thinking that the authorities would develop a scheme to catch them. So he took the initiative to go and talk to the bridge operator.

There were two men that operated the bridge. One was black and the other was white. The black man worked during the times that John and his crew vandalized the trains. John felt strongly about his role as the black Robin Hood, and he was confident that he could convince the bridge operator to open the bridge to allow them to cross when the authorities called. John understood the conditions that blacks were facing, so he approached the bridge operator by saying, "How are you today, Sir?" The bridgeman replied, "Well, Son, I'm doing just fine." When the bridgeman responded in a friendly manner, John asked him this question, "Mister, could you use some more food at home during these hard times?" He looked at John and said, "Sure, I could use anything extra that I can get, 'cause this white man's job just ain't doing it." So, when he spoke in this fashion, John began to tell him about his new role as the black Robin Hood. The bridgeman listened attentively. He said he had not heard anything like that before in his life. Nonetheless, he said it was a good idea. The conversation went over very well, and John agreed to bring him boxes of food in order to get him to keep the bridge open, while John and his crew ran across it with the goods. There was one flaw in the agreement. The bridgeman explained to John that he had only so much time before he had to close the bridge, and if they could not beat the time, he had to close the bridge or he would lose his job. John understood the situation, and he made sure that he and his crew got across the bridge in time. The vandalism took place for two years, and they never got caught. The bridgeman received his goods, and many poor people in Harlem went to bed without hunger. John wondered if anyone knew that his philanthropist food service was based on the movie "Robin Hood."

King Kong & Heroin

John described an almost lethal alcoholic beverage that was consumed by many in Harlem. It was bootleg liquor called "King Kong." King Kong was a predecessor of what is known today as PCP, Sherman, or Acid. A hallucinogenic beverage that caused many good men and women to fall, it was introduced into Harlem during the 1940's.

King Kong fascinated the users. Every week, he said, you would hear about someone jumping off a high-rise building, trying to fly. It was cheap, and anybody could make it, if they had the right ingredients. John says that the mob, crooked judges and police weren't earning money from the substance, and the people were killing themselves so regularly that it became a hazard. Therefore, the powers to be had to come up with a solution for this hazard and at the same time earn money from the users. Organized crime bosses held meetings, and they decided that they must introduce another kind of controlled substance for people because death destroys revenues and profits. So heroin was introduced into Harlem and other U.S. cities. It seemed like it happened overnight. The powers to be said, "The hell with King Kong."

John said that the people in Harlem didn't manufacture heroin. It comes from the poppy flowers that are grown in Middle Eastern countries like Iran. The U.S. controls the borders, but they refuse to stop the sale of heroin because there is much money to be earned.

I am not saying that all of the authorities are crooked, but what I am saying is that from my experience on the streets, I know of crooked cops, politicians, and clergy alike. Even today, the people in Harlem are so despondent from racism and economic degradation that any kind of escape is good to them.

In John's Junior High School days, there were many individuals from age ten on up that spiked heroin. John used to hang out with junkies after school and weekends to obtain information about this "shit called Heroin." He used to go up on the rooftops to watch how a person he knew changed into something or someone else. It was a sight to behold.

John wondered why, and how, the junkies could afford to purchase the dope. So he began to ask questions. The first thing one of them would say is, "Johnny, this shit here is the hell of Earth. Do you see these shopping bags that most junkies carry around on their arms?" John said, "Yes." He said, "Well, we feed our habits through these bags." On many occasions, junkies would go downtown to steal goods from the white merchants to support their habits. "If I didn't do that, I would be stealing from the people in Harlem because the white police in the white neighborhood would not allow us to walk around in their neighborhood due to the color of our skin. So basically that is the bottom line as to how junkies, like myself, feed our habits."

John asked, "What about jobs?" The junkie replied, "Some of us have jobs and we call those people professional junkies. They go to work each day, get off, and go feed their habit. A professional junkie is a person who walks around in the summertime with a long coat or long-sleeved shirt, while most other people will have on short everything. They wear these long clothes to cover up the tracks on their arms and legs."

During those days, parents looked out for all the neighborhood children, and somehow the word got back to John's father that he had been hanging around with junkies. When his father received the undesirable news, he sat him down and told him point blank that he was not to hang out with that kind of people. John had great respect for his father, and when he spoke to John in this tone, John's Adam's apple would tighten up and he could hardly breathe. In this case, his father's scare tactic didn't work because the junkies were certainly not going to force him to inject their dope, because they loved it too much.

John said that one of the funniest things he has seen in his life was two junkies fighting.

You know when two sober people fight, there is a lot of emotion, anger, and violence. Not with junkies! You see, when a junkie shoots up, there's a complete metamorphosis. They talk with a slurred speech, and they move in slow motion. When the first blow is thrown, one has time enough to go to the store, buy a sandwich, eat it, and come back to watch the first blow land. That is how slow those fools moved when they were using. Junkies loved Jazz too. For some reason or other you could always find them around the record stores in Harlem. They would be singing, moving, and grooving to the music. It seemed to take them into another dimension. I learned a lot from hanging out with junkies, and the most important thing I learned was that I never wanted to get caught up in "Hell on Earth."

The English Channel

One day, John heard a radio news report about a man swimming the English Channel. This news report was different because John did not know what the English Channel was. Wanting to know more about it, he went to his father and asked him what the English Channel was, and why did someone want to swim across it. His father told him that the English Channel is a channel between Southern England and Northern France. It is 350 miles long and 20 to 100 miles wide. Generally, the person that swam the channel swam between 20 and 24 miles across the width of the channel. John asked him if the person who swam it continued to swim until he finished, or what? His father answered, "yes." John's final question was, "What does a person get out of doing something like that?" His father answered, "A person receives personal satisfaction from the accomplishment. Secondly, he could swim it, establish a record, and be remembered."

During John's investigative talk with his father, he found out that his father could not swim. He told John that he swam "like a rock," -- he went straight to the bottom. The information that John received inspired him to join the YMCA to learn to become a swimmer.

Swimming came naturally to John. On many occasions when he was a small child, he had spent three or four hours playing in the water in the bathtub. He would pretend that he was a fish or some other water creature. The lessons from the YMCA paid off: by the time John finished Jr. High School he had become the two hundred meter freestyle city champion. In fact, he won his first medal ever in swimming. Again, on the radio during his freshman year of Junior High School, he heard about the Olympics. Remember now, there were few TV's around, so John asked his father what the Olympics was. Earl explained to him that it was an international sports competition held once every four years. John said, "I continued to ask, 'Well, how does one go?' Pop said, 'Each country has a competition between their best athletes, and those who qualify compete against others as representatives of their home country every four years in an Olympic competition.' " So John told his father, "I want to become the first black two hundred meter Olympic medal winner for the US swim team. I want to be the first because I have not heard of any black swimmers in the Olympics."

Inspired by his success in swimming John began to dream about using his abilities in other ways. He approached his father and inquired about how he could become an Olympic swimmer. As his father contemplated the question he saw a different side of his father. It was a serious and sad expression that John could see and hear in his father's voice when he said, "Son, if you plan to go to the Olympics, you will have to do it another way." John said, "What do you mean, Pop?" He looked at John with tears in his eyes and said,

Son, because of racial prejudice by the white man you cannot go to the Olympics as a swimmer. Swimming is a white man's sport, and because he is unable to have a natural skin color like yours, he hates and despises the color of your beautiful black skin. Therefore, he punishes us because God did not give him the thing that he wants the most, to have color. The white man will only allow you to compete in a sport where he knows that it is impossible for him to win. For example, he will allow you to box, run track and field, and now he will only allow a few to play in professional baseball. Anything outside of those sports, he will tell you that you are inferior by nature, when he knows damn well that the only thing that keeps all other blacks and non-whites from competing is economic and political control.

His broken dream, John looked into his father's eyes and began to think back to when his Uncle Luther took him to the beach when he was four or five years old. He recalls running and sliding in the sand, and he had caused some sand to blow on this white man. The white man grabbed him up fiercely and said, "Who let this little nigger on the beach!" John became very frightened, and the man let him go. He went and told his Uncle Luther what the guy had done and said. His Uncle Luther immediately went over to this guy to handle things. As I mentioned earlier, Uncle Luther was a man of great stature; he stood seven feet, two inches tall. Uncle Luther got up and walked over to the guy and got verbal and physical, saying, "Did you call him a nigger? Well that boy that you called a 'nigger' is my nephew, so, if you call him a nigger then I must be the same nigger. He is defenseless! Talk to me like you talk to him." John said his Uncle Luther "whipped this guy's ass," and told him that he would be back tomorrow. He told the guy that he had better not say anything when he returned.

John reflected on this incident, realizing that some white people treat and feel differently about black people.

His father Earl asked John, "Where would you train?" John said that he could train at the YMCA. Earl said that was impossible because the pool was set up for people to come in and cool off. He said that it was not possible to train in the Harlem River because many had drowned there. He said John could not train in the ocean due to rough currents. Lastly, he said that he could certainly not train in the white folks' facilities. John was hurt deep down in the core of his soul. Thinking about what his father had said, John said, "How can white people take away my dreams like that? It is not fair!" There was nothing that either his father or he could do, except to change his dream to something else. It took him quite some time to overcome the fact that America had turned his Olympic swimming dream into a nightmare. However, God was with him, and he decided to dream in the world of boxing.

Golden Gloves

John joined the Golden Gloves in 1958. He had all of the necessary skills that it took to be an excellent boxer. He had a great body, he was powerful and he had the ability to knock a person out with either hand. One can say that he was the Mike Tyson of his day. Boxing required one to purchase a cup, boxing gloves, mouth-piece, boxing shoes, and other things. John did not like the idea of asking his parents for money, so he told the trainers that if they desired him to box, they would have to find a way to finance what he needed. The trainers didn't have a problem with his request because they knew that he was worth the investment. John fought and trained to the point where he began to dream again, dreaming of becoming the heavyweight champion of the world, about even becoming a boxer for the Olympics. He knew that without a doubt he was good.

At the end of a year he had gained the respect of his trainers and his peers. He had a reputation on the streets, and he could hold his own with the best of them. Training hard every day, he looked forward to going to the gym. He used to watch various fighters, and he looked for various things that he could do to make himself a better fighter. Several of the fighters had their own styles, and at the same time, many of them used similar techniques. John was unique, for he could knock a guy out with either hand. He was extremely quick, strong, and elusive. He could hit a guy and move just as quick after he hit him. He loved to fight: both the art of fighting, and the challenge of out-thinking one's opponent in the heat of battle. It was a high for him, and he wanted to show the world that he was good, too. He had boxing on his mind all of the time. This was a great outlet for him. It kept him off the streets, and kept him focused. His friends would pump him up by saying how good he was. The coaches told him that he had a good chance at qualifying for the Olympics or even going pro. His father saw his enthusiasm, and he was proud of him. John's brothers, who were older, gave him their blessings, and they benefited from his reputation on the streets in terms of protection. The people in the projects and other neighborhoods knew not to mess with anyone in his family because he took care of business. It seemed that everyone was happy with his boxing success except his mother. She never said anything about it, until he got totally immersed in it. This is how she responded to his success.

One day after working out, John came home tired and ready to eat his mother's good cooking. He noticed that his mother was acting a little strange. She was looking at him in a very serious way, and she approached him with the kindest of words. "Johnny, you know that you are my baby boy, and I love you with all my heart. You have a very handsome face and the sport that you are participating in is very dangerous. I don't want to see my baby boy get hurt, nor do I want anyone to damage your pretty face. So, Johnny, Mama is asking you not to box anymore." As his mother was speaking to him in this motherly tone, he could hear the bombs and cannons bursting in his head all over again; he was bursting to tell his mother that he had established a reputation on the streets of Harlem, and he could certainly handle himself in the ring. Because of the respect that he had for her, however, he said, "Yes" to her request.

She was not satisfied with his answer. She took it a little further. She looked him directly in the eyes, into his soul, and said, "Johnny, I want you to promise Mama that you won't box anymore." He knew that his mother was serious, so he made a promise that he would not box anymore.

After agreeing not to box, he was "frustrated as hell," and his appetite left him. He had a million thoughts in his head, and he had no one to talk to but himself. He had put so much time and effort into boxing and to have it end this way was a great blow. What were the trainers, his friends, and others going to say? Moreover, how could a potentially great fighter with a reputation on the streets and in the gym tell the coach that his Mama didn't want him to box! He only had until the next day to think about all of these things, and to get up the nerve to tell the coaches that he couldn't box anymore. So the next day, John went to the gym to talk with the trainer. It was one of the hardest things that he ever did.

Although he had quit boxing, he enjoyed the sport tremendously. He monitored the boxers that he had trained with, especially his good friend, Emerald Griffith. Emerald was older than he was, and he went through the Golden Glove ranks to become professional. John said that he would never forget the fight that Emerald had with this boxer from Puerto Rico named Kid Barrett. Right before the fight began Kid made the mistake of calling Emerald a faggot. Almost immediately, Emerald got this vicious look upon his face, and he said out loud, "I am going to kill him." When John saw the look of death in Emerald's face, he instantly remembered that same expression when he had called Emerald a faggot when they were together on Jones Beach. John said that Emerald chased and pinned him to the ground saying, "John, don't you ever call me that name again." John said, "Hey man, I'm sorry." Emerald let him go.

The bell sounded, and both fighters met in the middle of the ring. Emerald threw some devastating punches to Kid's head; they brought some serious concerns to Kid's corner. Dominating each round, Emerald had hit Kid so many times in his head that by the fourth round it swelled up like a balloon. Kid was a defeated fighter, and he fell to the floor from a right punch that the entire crowd felt. He was breathing rapidly, and blood was everywhere. His head swelled so rapidly that he needed immediate attention. While the doctor and trainers began to work on him the stadium was quiet; the only voices one heard were the medical professionals in the ring. Everyone, including Emerald, was hopeful that Kid would pull through, but the prospect looked dim because the doctor began to drill a hole in Kid's head to release the pressure on his brain from the swelling. It was a gruesome sight that was hard to look upon.

Though the doctors tried everything to revive Kid, it was to no avail: he died in the ring. Emerald could not believe what had happened, and he confided to John that he never intended to kill him. He only tried to punish Kid for calling him a fag. He said that he was truly remorseful about killing him. After seeing the fight, John said that many things crossed his mind. He especially thought about his mother talking to him about the dangers of the sport. John still believed that he would have been one of the best boxers in the world, but that fight and his mother's wishes erased his dream of becoming a professional boxer.

Caterpillars

John and his family moved to the Harlem River Project, which housed one fifth of the population of Harlem. It had amenities such as playgrounds, picnic areas, a police force, benches where people could sit and socialize, and hundreds of beautiful trees. When the leaves on the trees flourished, hundreds of thousands of caterpillars would come out of nowhere to feast on the leaves and the people.

One day when John came home from school, he noticed that his mother was sitting in the window looking out, while many other people were outside sitting on the benches talking. He asked her why she didn't care to go out, and she said that she did not want to be bothered with the caterpillars because they were infectious. She said that if you hit a caterpillar and it burst, then the liquid would make you break out in a rash. John knew that she was right because it had happened to many of them in the past. After he spoke with his mother about this, he took the initiative to go and make a complaint to the project manager about the caterpillars.

I never looked at the situation as me being a child. I looked at the situation where some-thing was wrong and I wanted to make it right. I knew that those caterpillars were not sup-posed to be falling out of the trees con-sistently every year. I knew this, because my homies and I used to walk about two miles to go swim at High Bridge Pool, where the

Jews lived. When we got into their area, we saw guys using spray guns to spray the trees. In the High Bridge area there were no caterpillars to be found.

Therefore, John was wondering why the manager was not spraying their trees. All of this was going through his mind as he went to talk to the manager about the problem. When John arrived at the office, he confidently walked in. The manager, who was sitting down doing some paperwork, looked up and John asked him why they had problems with caterpillars. He looked at him and said, "What the hell are you doing in my office?" John took offense at what he said, and told him that he had the right to be there to make a complaint. The manager became defiant and told John to get out of his office. While he was telling him this, he pushed a button to call his henchmen or bodyguard. In less than no time, a black man walked into his office dressed in a gray uniform. John had seen him on many occasions, but his presence did not disturb him. As I mentioned, the project had its own city housing police force, and John knew that if he stayed there, he would have to deal with them. Therefore, he left, telling the manager that he had forty-eight hours to do something about the problem. The manager said, "What do you mean?" John replied, "Somebody better tell me something within forty-eight hours or I will take care of the problem."

He was dead serious about what he said, and after forty-eight hours had passed, John had not heard anything from anybody, so he went to the gas station and he purchased some gasoline. He walked back to the projects, and in his mind he was thinking about what he was going to do. He said that he had burning on his mind! He said that he had planned to set every tree on fire, and by the time he reached the projects, he was furious enough to do it. When he arrived at the projects, he selected a tree to burn, so that all could see. He told everyone (in a loud voice) to clear the area, saying, "I'm going to take care of the caterpillar problem. So get back!" He repeated it over again, saying, "Get back!" The area cleared, and he took the gasoline and he threw some on the bottom and top of a tree. He took a book of matches out of his pocket, struck a match and threw it on the gasoline-drenched tree. Poof! The tree went! Flames and smoke spread instantly, and John moved away quickly, as he watched the caterpillars burn.

The people in the project didn't know what to think. He said that he heard all kinds of comments as the people gathered around to see the fire show. Some shouted, "He's crazy, he's crazy!" While others screamed, "Call the fire department, call the police." John said that the people were calling him crazy, not knowing that he had tried to make a complaint to the project manager to correct the problem. In the meantime, John moved to the next tree, and again he told everyone to get back. He poured gasoline on a second tree, struck a match, and set it on fire. Smoke, flames, and the smell of burning caterpillars were in the air.

After he torched the second tree, the police and the fire department were driving towards the fire. John said that he could hear the sirens, but that did not deter him. He set the third tree on fire, and the police and the management began to run after him. John says that they were confused because they did not know whether to catch him or put out the fire. Finally, the police caught up with John, and they ordered him to put the gasoline can down and turn himself in. Obeying their commands, he surrendered to them. They took him into custody. John said that the police asked him many questions, and he responded with the story about the manager and what he had said to him about the caterpillar problem. The police were not impressed with his story, but John was a juvenile, and the police had to release him to his parents.

His parents were extremely disturbed about what he had done. The housing project tried to evict them from their home, and they pressed charges against John's folks for arson and destruction of property. This meant that John and his parents had a date set with the courts. But John didn't understand the seriousness of the problem. All he knew was that he saw a problem, and he used his best judgment to correct it. Mr. and Mrs. Carlos understood what John was trying to do, but at the same time, they explained to him what he did was wrong. John didn't care about going to court. He had told the manager that he was going to take care of the caterpillars, and he had.

A few days later John's parents received a letter from the court. The letter gave them information about what the charges were and when the trial date would be. His father had to get a lawyer, and things weren't looking too good. About two to three weeks after they received the letter, the trial began.

The Housing authorities made their opening statements, and the office manager spoke on the witness stand. He made several remarks, saying that John had threatened him, and he was very rude when he came to speak with him in his office. The manager also mentioned that an adult should have addressed the problem and not a child. He made other statements about arson, the destruction of property, and evicting them from their home. After the office manager spoke, John was placed on the stand. The judge looked down at him and said, "Young man, don't you know that what you did was a dangerous act?" And John responded, "Yes, but I made sure that I got everyone out of the way before I set the trees on fire. My intentions were not to hurt anyone. Sir, I went to the manager's office, and I asked him about the problem, and he threw me out because he felt that I, as a kid, had no business being in his office asking him about anything. I felt that I did have a right to ask him about the problem. I did not tell him the real reason why I asked him to get rid of the problem, and that is the fact that I saw my mother sitting in the window afraid to come outside because she did not want to deal with the caterpillars."

John also mentioned the fact that the High Bridge area didn't have caterpillars. Then he asked the court, "Why does High Bridge Housing have money to spray their trees and we don't? Is it because we're black?" The judge said, "Very good questions." He then asked the manager, "Does your project receive subsidies to spray the trees?" The manager replied, "Yes." He had some other explanation as to why the trees hadn't been sprayed. The judge became upset over the fact that the project had not been sprayed, and he immediately made a judgment on the case. The judge said, "John, I want you to know that what you did was wrong, and you could have caused some serious damage to person and property. If you have some concerns with anything, you must talk to your mom and dad, your pastor, the police or someone that you trust to help you solve your problems. If this kind of conduct occurs again, there could be some serious consequences. At the same time, Son, I want to say that you are quite a fighter, and I want you to know that we are going to solve this caterpillar problem today."

The judge looked over at the manager, and said, "Sir, it is because of the way you treated this lad that he felt compelled to go to such extremes to get his point across, in order to get the caterpillar situation straightened out. He wanted to see his mother go out and socialize with others, and because of your negligence not to use the subsides to spray the trees, Mrs. Carlos and others chose not to go outside. Today, I am ruling in favor of the Carlos family. The court orders the Harlem River Projects to use the subsidies to spray the trees, and if it does not come into compliance with the stipulations that govern the subsidies immediately, criminal charges will be held against the project management. I am dismissing the arson case against John and the Carlos family, and the Harlem River Projects does not have the privilege to evict them. Case closed!" After the court order, the Harlem River Project began spraying the trees, and in time, the caterpillar problem was no more.

Now it was the last month of John's Junior High School year. He had gone through many trials in his short life. He had been kicked out of elementary school because he was rebellious against a racist school system that refused to teach black students about their heritage. He became Harlem's black Robin Hood when he stole from the rich and gave food to the poor. He'd nearly burned down the projects because of a caterpillar problem. And losing his dream of swimming to racism

81

had traumatized him, and he had given up his boxing career because he was his mother's baby boy, and she did not want him to damage his handsome face.

In time, he became bored because he did not have anything to occupy his time. Therefore, he and his crew got together and they began to vandalize the trains again. He became a thug for both right and wrong reasons. In between the vandalism, they went to Pile Park on the weekends, where the track meets took place. At that time, the runners didn't have locker rooms to lock their clothes up. The track participants had to roll their clothes up and leave them on the sidelines where thieves (like John and his crew) could come and steal them. Personally, John was not interested in running track. He was there only to steal clothes and whatever else was around.

News of their breaking and entering got around, and one day two black detectives that John's father had known came over to him after a track meet. Lester and Bryant were detectives from the 32nd Precinct on 135th Street, between 7th and 8th Avenues, well known in both the black and white communities. Mr. Lester was around six feet tall, stocky, light-skinned man with salt and pepper hair. Mr. Bryant was a bit shorter than Mr. Lester, standing five feet nine inches tall, a brown-skinned man with a stocky build. They approached John and his crew. The boys knew who the detectives were, and Mr. Lester began by saying that some people had been breaking in various places, and they had a good idea who it was. He continued that it would be just a matter of time before they caught them. After he finished telling them the bad news, Detective Lester looked at John and said, "Son, you may not have realized it yet, but you have a talent." John said, "What do you mean I have a talent?" The detective replied, "You're a runner!" John started laughing because he thought that everyone in Harlem could run. He thought, "Shit, I have seen guys snatch black women's purses and the women would chase them down and take their purse back."

When Mr. Lester heard John laugh, he slapped him across his head so hard that he can still feel it today. That blow got John's attention very quick, and Mr. Lester said to him, "Boy, I am serious about what I am saying." He said, "Get on that track, and run until I tell you to stop." John got started running immediately, and Mr. Lester got caught up with something else. He forgot about him for about an hour and a half. By the time it dawned on John that Mr. Lester had forgotten about him, he had run twelve to fifteen miles. Mr. Lester returned and called John off to the side. John was huffing and puffing from the long run, and he wondered what more Mr. Lester wanted. He began to tell John about the exciting world of track and field. John listened attentively while he regained his breath. After the brief lecture, Mr. Lester urged John to join a track team before he got himself in trouble with the law. It was from that point on that John became interested in running track and field. Mr. Lester really convinced him that he had a talent for running. He began to run for the New York Pioneer Club where he was an instant success, and the coaches, fans, his peers, and his seniors knew that he would develop into a great track runner.

Before John graduated from Jr. High, there was a mix-up about where he would attend school. He wanted to attend Manhattan Technical and Vocational High School, because he wanted to swim for them. But on the day that he was to confirm that decision, he ditched school!

John's reputation for running quickly was known by many in his Jr. High school, and someone in the office knew that Manhattan Technical and Vocational High School did not have a very good track team. So the office person decided to change John's decision by switching his records to Herron High, where there was an excellent track team. John knew nothing about Herron, but a few of his friends told him that Herron had a swimming program. John graduated from Frederick Douglas Jr. High School in June of 1961, thinking that he was soon going to be swimming for medal competition. He practiced all summer long, but when the school year came around he would get some disheartening news.

4

High School Days

Track and Field Beginnings

On opening day in September of the year 1961, the 16 year old freshman, John Carlos, awakened around six o'clock in the morning to prepare to attend his new High School. The High Schools in New York require four years of study to graduate. John was excited about seeing what his new school had to offer him. He got up and dressed himself, and he could smell the food on the table. Mrs. Carlos prepared breakfast for the family, and they ate heartily. John had already learned how to catch the buses and trains. He was eager to obtain some information about the swim team. So, when he arrived at school, the first thing that he did was to ask someone about it. It was a comical situation because the person that he asked said, "Man, we don't have a pool, let alone a swim team." John became disturbed about the response to his question, and he was upset with his friends who had lied to him. He thought about all of the times that he spent swimming to prepare himself during the summer. This was a big disappointment for him.

John's ability to run and be a thug had preceded him. The principal, teachers and the coaches had heard from the newspaper or his school confidential file about his ability to run. This caused some conflict for John from day one. He was prejudged by all. While John was trying to get himself acquainted with his new environment, it would be a matter of a few days before he encountered the track and field coach, Mr. Dearson. Coach Dearson stood six feet, five inches. He looked like a boxer from the old school. He was low key, but he would speak his mind. Their meeting was quite negative.

Coach Dearson did not have much to say to John. When he told him point blank that he thought that he was too much of a gangster to run for his program, John understood. Further, it was not important that he run track anyway. Basically, he got familiar with his new school, and found out where he fit in.

The Chicken Protest

John was not used to being around a diverse student population. He called it the "Salad Bowl." A mix of Jews, Caucasians, Italians, African-Americans, Puerto Ricans and other ethnicities, it was in great contrast to what he had experienced in Elementary and Junior High School. Nonetheless, everyone seemed to get along under the circumstances. There was no racial tension at all!

After a few months, a problem arose. It had nothing to do with ethnicity or race; it had to do with the food they served in Herron's cafeteria. They were selling the students chicken that had not been cleaned and prepared properly. Students would find feathers still in the chicken, and sometimes it was not cooked well. On top of that, the school fed them chicken every day! John said, "The menu had chicken soup, chicken salad, chicken sandwiches, chicken gumbo, baked chicken, broiled chicken, fried chicken, chicken pot pie, chicken cacciatore, chicken and dumplings, chicken gizzards, and chicken liver. The chicken never had a day off." They were chickened out!

Many students were upset about the poor food service. The bad food was the talk around the campus. John had talked to many students who had had enough, and yet they were not doing anything about it. Therefore, John decided to go to the principal and ask him why the cafeteria did not clean and prepare the food properly. On the way to the principal's office John thought about what he was going to say. When he arrived, he asked the secretary if he could conference with the principal, and she arranged for him to go in to speak with him. He sat down patiently and waited for a few minutes, then he was directed into the principal's office. The principal was a white man who had a friendly personality, and he seemed easy to talk to. They spoke to each other, and the principal asked him how he might assist him.

John approached the situation like a man, and asked, "Why aren't the cafeteria staff cleaning and preparing the food properly? Everyone is complaining about the food, and many of them have found chicken feathers in the chicken." The principal's attitude changed altogether, and he looked at John with anger saying, "You have no right to confront me about the food in the cafeteria. Who do you think you are?" He replied boldly, "I'm John Carlos, and I do have a right to ask you about the poor food service." The conversation stopped immediately! The temperature in the room got hot, and the principal responded angrily saying, "Get out of my office." John got to his feet, and he walked towards the door and said with temerity, "You have forty-eight hours to correct the problem, or we will correct it." The principal asked, "What do you mean, we will correct it?" John simply stated again, "You have forty-eight hours to correct it." He never answered the question. He walked out of the office. The next day, the same thing occurred, the food was not prepared right. The next day the same thing again. On the third day, John took action! He put the word out that everyone was going to brown bag it. He spoke with the Italians, Puerto Ricans, African-Americans, and Jews. Then he sent his crew out and they spread the word to the different groups. All communication was done by word of mouth. They were all for it, and the "Brown Bag Boycott" began. There were at least ten to fifteen thousand students that he had to communicate with, and he made it plain that everybody had better brown bag it. In less than two days, the strike was on.

John always had a group of guys around him who followed his leadership. So, he instructed them to stop students who decided to continue to buy lunch. John said that the students who bought food from the cafeteria would be walking to their seats to eat, and somehow, they would have an accident. There were so many accidents that eventually the students got the message, and they began to brown bag it. John's crew were not bullies; they established a mission, and they carried it out.

The boycott went on for 8 days. The school was losing thousands of dollars, and the principal came looking for John. In their first encounter, the situation became intolerable for the principal, but now that it was a matter of dollars and cents, the principal was forced to deal with him. John said that the principal did everything in his power to intimidate him, but it was to no avail.

John had three demands. First, he demanded that the cafeteria clean and prepare the chicken properly. Secondly, he demanded that the cafeteria create a new menu. Thirdly, he demanded that the principal treat him like a man. The principal sat and listened to John's demands, and as John put it, "He got pissed off again." When he could take no more, he ordered him to leave his office. John left! In time, he knew that the principal would ask him to return.

One day passed. Then another. On the tenth day, John returned to the principal's office, and he said, "I am going to take this matter to the press and expose this problem to the public." John said that when the message about going to the press hit the principal's ears, they turned as red as an apple. Reluctantly, he was ready to talk. He asked John to return to his office, and he said defeatedly, "If you call your guys off, I will take care of the food problem." An agreement was made, and John made sure that the principal met all of his demands. The principal immediately called his cafeteria staff and held a meeting. He ordered them to prepare and clean the chicken properly, and incorporate different kinds of food on the menu. He also gave John the respect that he was due by not kicking him out of his office. He allowed him to remain there until they came to a full understanding. John left the principal's office in triumph, and he immediately put the word out to call off the brown bag boycott. The next day, when the students saw a difference in their food, John was proud of what they had accomplished. The boycott taught him to fight for what was right, despite what the authorities say.

John became "the man" at Herron High, and before long, he got himself involved in some trouble. He was not attending his classes, doing his classwork, and he was accused of being involved in some fights. His bad habits came to the attention of the principal and the Dean of Students, Mr. Silverman, and it was necessary to call his mother in for a conference. On the conference date, the principal explained to Mrs. Carlos that her son was a terrible student. Mr. Silverman was there, too. He talked about John's negativity in such a way that it caused Mrs. Carlos to break down and cry. John was Mrs. Carlos' heart, and to hear someone talk about him in this way was unbearable. John, on the other hand, could not stand to see his mother cry, and he got angry and shouted, "The meeting is over." Everything stopped in an instant, and John asked his mother not to cry. After giving attention to her, he looked at the principal with the look of death while he escorted his mother out of the office. John said the principal sat there looking stupid saying, "I'm sorry, Mrs. Carlos."

John was permitted to return to school the next day. On this particular day, he arrived at school with his right hand man, Willie. Willie was a hard-core, tall, strong, and powerful individual, who would lose his cool and beat someone's ass at a whim. He had little or no regard for common sense. He did things, giving no thought to them. The one good thing John said about Willie was that he was loyal. When they were out on the streets being confronted by others, he was always ready to fight. In fact, Willie would not allow John to fight with certain individuals. He would step in and say, "You don't have to do this. I will handle it." John said that it was somewhat nice to have a guy like this around, and at the same time John could teach him wisdom and self-control.

John and Willie were walking to class, and Mr. Silverman stopped him in order to talk. He began with some derogatory statements about the manner in which John's mother had handled the meeting. This rather pissed John off, but he continued to listen to Mr. Silverman who stated that he did not like the things that John was doing at his school, and he would be very happy to see him leave and go elsewhere. Dean Silverman made a mistake by saying this in front of his man, Willie, because Willie got more upset about the situation than John did. By the time Mr. Silverman got through saying

derogatory things about John and his mother, Willie was
steaming mad.

During those days, the fire department had an ax
placed behind a glass window in case of a fire. Willie
broke the glass, swearing obscenities from the top of his
lungs saying, "I'm going to kill you, you motherfucker."
The Dean was a chunky man, but when Willie broke the
glass and got the ax, he broke off into a sprint that
deserved some merit. Willie chased the dean, and John
chased Willie to make sure that he didn't kill him.
Several of the teachers looked out of their rooms to see
what was going on. However, when they saw that ax
coming, they shut their doors immediately. They could
hear Willie saying, "I'm going to kill you." John caught
up with Willie, and he talked him down. He said in a
commanding voice, "Let it go, Willie. Cool it!" Willie
responded, and John took the ax away from him. The
Dean was relieved, but now he had his opportunity to do
what he wanted to do with John, and that was to get him
out of his school. Willie spared the Dean serious injury,
and he kept himself out of doing prison time. By the
time the commotion was settled, the police came and
arrested Willie for assault and battery on a teacher. And
Dean Silverman and the principal got their wish: John
was expelled in the middle of his sophomore year in 1962.

He was transferred to the Manhattan Technical
and Vocational High School which had been his choice in
the first place. His reputation for running and being a
gangster had preceded him there, too. In the back of
John's mind, he had an interest in running track. One
day, during the beginning of the 1963-64 season, a track
runner named Stanley Beachem came to him, explaining
how he had broken his arm. After he explained the

situation, John said "Man, you only broke your arm, you can still run!" Stanley replied, "Yes, you're right, and I am going to run." Now during that time John was still drinking wine and clowning around. It wasn't long after that when another incident occurred where a track runner named Victor broke his leg. This time the track coach got in touch with John, and asked him to run. John agreed! Coach Youngermen asked John to report to his office the next day for training. John, in turn, asked the coach where the track field was, and he stated, "There isn't one." John asked, "Well, where do we train?" Coach Youngermen explained to John that they trained in the hallways of the school. The coach had set up stations where the team ran through the corridors of the school, and to complete the track, they would use tables on the outside of the building. The set up was rather strange, but he made a decision to train and learn as much as he could.

The first track meet that John participated in was the Bishop Lockery Invitation. Several schools were represented there from all over the city. Almost every team had a powerhouse! The invitation had two areas to classify runners. The first area of classification was for those who had run and placed. These individuals were placed in what was called the "open event." The second area was classified for novices or rookies or for those who had never competed. John was classified as a rookie in the competition. Although everyone was classified in different categories, everyone competed against one another.

With hysteria in the air the competitors were preparing themselves for competition by stretching and doing light jogs. Students and spectators waited patiently to see how well their schools would do in each track event. While this was occurring, the coach came over and said to John, "If you get in fourth place, maintain your position. That will be fine." Then he left to do something. When John heard him say that he jumped up and said, "Well, why does he have us here? He honestly doesn't believe that we can win. I don't want to run for this man." He grabbed his bag to put some things away, but his teammates begged him to stay. He thought about it for a moment, and remained there. However, he couldn't get his mind off what Coach Youngblood had said. John said that the coach had no concept of what track and field was all about. He was teaching track to earn extra money and nothing more.

The track meet was held at an armory. The track field was flat, having no round curves like a normal track field, so the authorities used pieces of wood that curved to make the track go in a circle. All of the participants were sitting on the inside of the flat track. The competition began with the hundred-yard dash. Some of the guys ran with tremendous speed. The next event was the two hundred-yard dash, and they ran just as fast. There were several other events going on while the fast running took place. There was the long jump, high jump, and the pole vault. John could see the tension that was building up in his teammates after they witnessed each race. Nevertheless, John had no fear! The guys were talking about how fast everyone was running, and they were psyching themselves out. As tension continued to build, John spoke up:

Fellows, listen up! We did not come here to lose! We can beat these guys! I am not a loser;

> I was born to win! I am in the best shape of my
> life, and no one out here is going to defeat John
> Carlos. The only reason the runners appear
> to run so fast is because we are sitting here
> looking at them. We're either just as fast or
> faster. When we run the relay, get me the
> baton anywhere near the pack, and I guarantee
> you that we will win. I will run the teams down
> like black folks in Texas run down rabbits.

They all looked and listened to him speak with the
greatest of confidence. They forgot what they had seen
and they focused their attention on what he was saying.
They were fired up, and they responded with a loud,
"Yeah!" To conclude, John said, "We are going to show
the coach what we're made of." They knew that he was
fast and it was possible that he could do what he said.
They began to believe in what he was saying. He told
each one of them that they had the ability to win. After
he spoke, they calmed down and exuded confidence,
saying, "Right on, John! We can do it!"

The mile relay would be easy for John to run,
except for one thing; he did not have the experience of
running the turns. The time came for them to begin the
race, and John was continuing to tell his teammates to be
cool and run. In a matter of minutes, the public schools
would find out who he was. John and his teammates
lined up in their lanes. The officials got the runners in
position, "Runners, on your marks, get set. . . " Then the
gun sounded. The first runner got off to a good start,
and he ran a good race. The other two did equally as
good. His teammates did everything right, and they
passed the baton to him at the right time. He ran the

pack down and won the race, breaking the school record. After the race, John called the guys over and said to them, "Now we are the top dogs." He didn't have to say much more because the victory proved its point. The coach became a believer, too, and from that point on, many eyes were looking their way.

After the morning events, they had lunch and everyone returned to continue the meet. Every school had a song, except for Manhattan Technical and Vocational School. But that situation did not last long because during lunch, many of the cheerleaders made up a song about how John and his team kicked ass by breaking the school's mile relay track record. During the afternoon races, the runners knew that they had to do well again, and they did. They broke their own record in the mile relay! They had established a reputation and a following at that track meet. The pressure was on them because many wanted to see if they were lucky, a fluke, or good.

The uniforms that the team wore were uniformed to the max, and John did not want to look like everyone else. So, he created his own uniform by sewing two large letters on the left and right cheeks of his running shorts. The letters spelled "J-C" in bright red letters. He did that, so that when people saw him run, they would know that it was him. After some time, John found out that the people were paying to come see him run. He was turned on because the people were turned on to him.

John ran the mile relay and the quarter mile for a very short time. He was comfortable with his role, until he discovered that the girls like the sprinters best. John loves the girls, and this quickly influenced his decision to run as a sprinter. He began running the one hundred yard dash, two hundred yard dash, and the sprint relay. He had an excellent track and field season during his junior year, becoming an all-city champion track and field star.

By the time he reached his senior year in the 1964-65 track season he had become better at his craft. He did not run for high school that year due to poor attendance and low grades, but he continued to run for the New York Pioneer Club because he had been running for them for the past three years. He and other participants received recognition and great exposure in New York State and New Jersey. The competition was king. He saw how the attendance increased as he dominated each race. The people were there to see him perform, and he knew it. Thus, he began to look at track and field as a business. He instructed his crew to bet on him to win. According to John, almost everyone in Harlem and America was betting on something. He knew that every school had a favorite runner and spectators would be willing to bet on their man against him. John told his homies not to worry about losing because he was sure to win. They seldom were disappointed.

Although John earned an excellent reputation in track and field, his classwork suffered due to poor attendance and dyslexia. After school, he continued to hang out with his homies, stealing here and there, chasing the women, drinking alcohol, and smoking a little weed. His reputation in track gave him celebrity status, and the women were after him. He was adored by many of them, and he could choose as he pleased

In 1963, John met a young lady by the name of Karen Benjamin Groce, the love of his life. It was rather curious the way they met. John was swimming at Pile

Park Pool with a friend. They were discussing what they wanted to do with their lives, and for some reason or another, John told his friend, "The next girl that walks out the girls' locker room door is going to be my wife." In less than one minute, Karen walked out the locker room door with her younger sister. He said that when he laid eyes on her, her total beauty and karma hooked him. He said that he immediately walked over to her and introduced himself, and from that point on, it was history. They dated for a year and a half. Then on February 29, 1965, John and Karen got married at Saint Charles Catholic Church in Harlem. There was no honeymoon because they did not have the money to afford one. They did manage to get a small apartment with all the basic necessities because Karen worked as a secretary. Nevertheless, nothing changed with him. He remained wild as wild could be.

Finally, his bad habits on the streets came to the attention of his mother. One day after a track meet, his mother began to talk to him about life and the things that he was doing. "Son, you are heading for a lifetime career in jail." His response was: "Mama, you may have a vision about a 'Johnny' being in jail, but you have the wrong Johnny." His mother lectured him several times, but he was sure that he was not going to jail. As a matter of fact he got a job, working for Montgomery Wards Company. The company was located in a large building in downtown Manhattan, on the tenth floor. After he worked a few months, John saw how the company earned millions of dollars shipping expensive goods to affluent clients, and he said to himself, "This company is not paying me enough for what I am doing." Again, he recognized that the rich were served and the poor were not, and he began thinking about his Robin Hood days. Stealing dresses was quite simple; he wrapped some up and dropped them out of the window on the thirteenth floor and down to the alley. After work, he picked them up, and he took them to Harlem to sell. John stole hundreds of dollars' worth of expensive dresses; he sold them cheaply for five dollars each. If a person didn't have the money, he would give them a dress and say, "Happy Birthday."

John stole dresses every month, and the company became aware of his activities. They began to watch him, and they set him up for the bust. On the day that he was caught, New York was experiencing a snowstorm. He was on the thirteenth floor, where he made the clothes drop. He headed for the tenth floor by elevator, to clock out, but the elevator didn't stop until he reached the first floor. Moreover, for some reason or another, he had a hunch that the police were upstairs, and something told him to leave. He looked at all of that snow outside, and he said, "No way in hell am I going to face that snow without my winter coat and hat." John thought about the situation again, and went with his first decision. He pushed the button for the tenth floor. As soon as he got close to the office, two police officers approached, grabbed his arms, and told him that he was under arrest. Then, one of the officers said to him, "You didn't kill anyone, so everything will be all right." He repeated, "Since it wasn't murder, you will get out."

The policemen allowed John to get his coat and hat, and they proceeded downstairs to the paddy wagon. The city of New York was celebrating Saint Patrick's Day, and to his surprise, there was a group of drunk Irishmen and black winos waiting to be arrested. There was a big commotion among both groups as to who was going to be in control while they all got into the paddy wagon. John did not know why, but for some reason one of the officers took his badge off and pinned it on the chest of one of the black winos. John said that the wino with the badge kicked one of the Irishmen in the ass. When he did that, all hell broke loose. John said it was like watching a comedy at the movies.

The wino deputy sheriff was talking nothing but shit, in a slurred voice, "God damn it! I'm the Sheriff, and don't none of you green-wearing, red-faced, leprechauns say shit to me. Just get your asses in the paddy wagon. And you nappy-head motherfuckers better not say shit either." While he was talking to everyone, the Irish and Negro winos were talking shit to each other. They were pushing and shoving each other. Small fights broke out, but no one seemed to get hurt. During this time, the officers were laughing their asses off at all of the antics. It was very funny to John, too, until the arresting officer told him that he had to get in with them. He told the officer that he was not about to get in there with them. He told him that he was not drunk, and he mentioned to the officer that he was too young to ride with all of those old men. The other officer agreed, and they placed John in a cage between the wagon and the front seat. The winos fought, cussed, and fussed all the way to the station. When they arrived at the station, the officers unloaded all of them. They placed John and everyone in the drunk tank. The place was packed, and John walked in, sat upon the heater, and watched more antics.

In the tank, there stood a man who was six feet, seven inches tall. John said this man had muscles from his neck to the bunions in his feet. He was as black as a shoe, and meaner than a motherfucker. He talked shit and fucked with everyone that didn't have that don't-fuck-with-me look on their face. John said, "This big dude walked over to a guy and asked him for a cigarette. The guy said that he didn't have one. So, the big guy commenced kicking this dude's ass. He kicked the dude's ass for a few minutes and he said, 'When I ask you for a cigarette, and you don't have one, you are supposed to get up off your ass and go hustle me one.'"

After he said that, he commenced to whuuping his ass again. Then he stopped and asked the guy for a cigarette again, and this time, the guy did exactly what the big guy told him to do. He went around to hustle cigarettes, and immediately after that, this monster of a guy began to fuck with everybody again. The guy came towards John, and he looked him dead in the eye. John did not show any fear, but he damn sure was concerned because if he had to he might have acted crazier than the big guy. They stared down at each other, and from the unemotional way John looked at him, he backed down. He continued to harass the weak, and before the authorities came, he went right back to beating the first guy that he started with. Eventually, the police came to see what was going on, and for some reason, the officers began to harass the guy that had already been beaten.

John's parents got him out of jail, and later he had to go to court. He had experienced court proceedings when he burned the caterpillars in the trees, but this time it would be different. He was stealing as the black Robin Hood, and also for personal gains. This time, the judge might not have been merciful. On his court date, he went before the judge who asked if he had been in trouble before, and he said, "No." Then he asked why he had been stealing dresses from the company. John told the judge that the company was selling the merchandise for large amounts of money, and they were not paying him enough money. He also told the judge that he was stealing the dresses and selling them for five dollars to the poor people in Harlem. John told him that if anyone did not have the money, he gave the dresses to them.

The judge looked at him, and he just could not believe what he had said. The judge saw John's sincerity, and it was a plus in his favor. The judge asked him why he tried to steal two dresses when the detectives caught him. John told him that he was going to sell one and give the other one to his wife because he had just gotten married. John concluded by telling the judge that he wanted her to look good for him. He said that he didn't know why he felt so relaxed in the courtroom. Maybe it was what the detective had said to him during the arrest. The judge inquired about John's background. After he checked his records, the judge looked down from the bench, and said, "I like the idea of what you were doing, but son, you are going to have to find a better way to help the poor because you are breaking the law. I have decided to drop the case, and I don't want to see you in my court again." John almost pushed his luck by asking the judge, "Your Honor, do you know who my favorite hero is?" The judge said, "No!" John said, "Robin Hood, because he didn't mind stealing from the rich and giving to the poor." The judge looked at him and shook his head, and he shouted, "Case dismissed!" John was grateful to the judge for giving him a chance to redeem himself. He also thought about what his mother had said to him about making jail his home. This was a great experience for John because he made up his mind that he did not want to spend any time in jail. From that time on, John gave up his lifestyle of crime to do good. He graduated from High School in January of 1965. He was 19 years old.

On November 9, 1965, New York City had a blackout: not a light in the city. That night Karen went into labor. John said that he had to get his wife, her belongings, and transportation to get to the hospital. He had a difficult time getting her there, but they made it. The hospital wasn't as prepared as they wanted to be, but they took care of everything. The next morning on November 10th Kimmy Carlos was born. John said that it was one of the happiest days of his life. When John and I discussed Kimmy, the first thing that came out of his mouth was, "That's my baby."

5

Trinidad

First Flight

In January of 1966 the indoor track and field season began. Track and field events were conducted all over New York State, but the ultimate event took place in the Madison Square Garden Arena in February. There John first got a chance to run against the leaders and legends of track and field, as a representative of the New York Pioneer Club. He was the young, little, snotty nose boy--the new kid on the block. The track meet had participants like the great Bob Hayes, Sam Perry, Charlie Green, and Mel Penter. John ran against these competitors in various heats, and he made it to the finals. When he ran against the legends in the finals, he placed last. Although he had finished last, he said that it was an honor to have competed with the best.

Immediately after the event, two coaches, Joe Yance and Ed Leavy, from the New York Pioneer Club, approached him, congratulating him on his performance. Very interested in boosting John's track career, they began to ask him questions about what he wanted to do in track and field. He expressed his interest in possibly running track for a college or university. Impressed with his answer, they asked him if he would like to go on a trip. John responded, "Yes, but where?" Mr. Yance asked John if he had heard of Trinidad, and if he knew where it was. John had never heard of it nor did he know where it was. They asked John to obtain a passport, and they would provide him with the other things that he needed to take an international trip. He was very excited about the offer. He told Mr. Yance and

Mr. Leavy that he would talk to his father about everything, and then he would contact them the next day.

John went home to his apartment and told Karen about the trip to Trinidad. He had inquired about taking his wife with him, but it was not possible due to limited funds. He explained to her that it was a two-week trip, and he would return home soon. Later that evening, he went to his father's house to ask him questions about the trip. Earl, promising that he would answer his questions the next day, decided to take John to the library to enlighten him. The next morning, John and Earl walked to the library, where Earl went and got a globe. He took his time and found Trinidad. He showed John New York and ran his finger to Trinidad. John discovered that Trinidad is an island in the West Indies. He said, "How in the world are we going to ride in a car or train to Trinidad?" His question was naive, but he had been accustomed to riding the train to various track meets across the state. Because he was underage, John asked his father if he could go. His father said, "Yes." It was imperative that John obtain a passport, so Earl took John downtown to city hall to purchase one. After they completed their business in city hall, John took the train to the Pioneer Club, and Earl returned to his shoe repair shop.

After he arrived at the club, he talked to Mr. Yance and Mr. Leavy; they told him that he had to go to the Amateur Athletic Union (AAU) in New York City. He went down there the next day and he met Dan Ferris and Owen Castle who explained the details of the trip. They said they were proud to have him as a representative for the AAU, and the trip was a good opportunity for him to get exposure in the track and field world. Both men were very cordial, and he listened attentively to what they had to say. After the meeting, they took John into a room and tailored him. John said that they gave him two pairs of slacks, two shirts, a Parker sport coat, a pair of Hush Puppies, toiletries, suntan lotion, a comb that only Elvis Presley could use, and a host of other things that were not conducive to what black people would wear or use in everyday life. John was not excited about receiving these things, and he could not understand why they did not have anything ethnic. As he received each product, he made comments like, "Man, black people don't wear Hush Puppies. Does it really look like I need a tan? This comb was made for Elvis and the people on the TV show *Route 66*." He made so many comments that it brought awareness that the AAU needed to find black products for their athletes. John also questioned the older black athletes that participated as to why they never complained about the products. None of them could give him a good reason, but as you can see, John spoke his mind.

In about three days, John was boarding a Pan Am airplane to Trinidad. Never having been on an airplane before, he was uncomfortable. When he left New York, it was below zero, and there were no clouds in the sky. The captain told the passengers that they were going to fly to San Francisco before leaving the United States. John had never been in California, and most people in the East knew California for its sunshine. When they arrived in California, it was cloudy, cold, and raining, so murky and cold that John decided not to get off the plane during the brief layover. The plane refueled in an hour, and they were off to Trinidad. The plane took off, and rose through the clouds. He did not know that the sun shone above the clouds; it was an amazing scene. He was still uncomfortable with flying, and in his discomfort, he began to check out things. The first thing he noticed was how beautiful the stewardesses were, never minding the fact that they were all white. John had on a real sweet Parker jacket that an elderly woman complimented him on, and from that compliment, the two engaged in conversation. She noticed that he was new at flying, so she tried to comfort him as much as possible through conversation. His stomach was upset, his armpits were full of sweat, and he responded to every little movement of the plane. The stewardess served them coffee, tea, and other things during the flight. At the time the stewardesses did not use carts to bring the food but carried it on trays.

John had never heard of a thing called turbulence, but when he encountered it, it was a rude awakening. They were flying about 30,000 feet when all of a sudden the plane dropped. The plane seemed to have dropped a thousand feet, and on top of that, the waitress near him panicked, throwing her tray filled with everything imaginable all over the place. You could hear screams and shouts of sheer terror. Then, to John's surprise, the woman that was trying to comfort him pulled her rosary beads out. John murmured to himself, "Shit, you know what that means!" The stewardesses were running down the aisles in a state of confusion. He panicked! All John could think of was getting over to a window seat to see what was going on. He looked out the window, and the most devastating thought hit him; he was thinking that if they were to crash and everyone on the plane perished except the old lady and him, how could he tell someone where he was especially if the old lady didn't know geography. Education became very real to John from that moment on!

John said that at that point his mind reflected back to his geography class when his teacher asked him to go to the board to tell the class where a particular place was on the map. He used to say to himself, "Why do I need to know where those places are? I will never visit them! All I need to know is where the Cotton Club, Yankee Stadium, or the Savoy is located. I don't need to know where anything else is!" He had no idea where they were. He said to himself, "This is a hell of a way to have to think serious about education." He was not talking about being a scholar. He was talking about having enough education to function in society.

Finally the plane came through the turbulence and everything returned to normal, and the old lady and John calmed down enough to resume their discussion. After many hours the plane landed in Antigua, in the West Indies. They stopped there to refuel, and the layover was about two hours. Before everyone got off the plane, John looked out the window and he saw a heavenly sight that prompted him to want to leave the plane as quickly as possible. The passengers got the go ahead signal from the captain, and John rushed to the front of the plane to get his duffel coat because he wanted to be the first one off the plane. However, in his haste, he did not notice that no one had a coat on except him. He remembered leaving a very cold New York and San Francisco.

John had his coat on when the stewardess opened the door, and the heat and humidity hit him "like a ball being hit out of Yankee Stadium." He turned around, looking at the people that he had pushed and shoved to get to the front and wanted to say, "Why didn't someone tell me?" It was embarrassing! As he took his coat off and deplaned, he noticed a sight that will remain in his mind for as long as he lives: black people of many shades.

John could not believe his eyes. The women were extremely beautiful, with breasts that stood lovely and firm. Their silky black hair flowed down their backs like the currents in the sea. Many of them wore no bras, and they all seemed to blend in with the surroundings. Their voices were different, and he wanted to learn as much as he could about these people. However, it was not possible because he only had two hours before leaving for Trinidad. He spent about an hour and a half mingling before they boarded the plane, and he said to himself that if Trinidad is anything like Antigua, they were in for a treat.

When they arrived in Trinidad, the officials there came out to greet them. The Americans were considered the powerhouses of track and field, and they had several outstanding athletes onboard, including Adolf Plumber (the world record holder in the four hundred meters), Ron Whitney, and Jerry Buckner. Adolf was different from all, except John. He smoked Winston cigarettes, drank, and involved himself in other vices. John didn't smoke cigarettes, but he did everything else, so they were a lot alike. John soon lost interest in the official business and focused his attention on the people.

Trinidad was like Antigua, except it was a whole lot better. John thought he had died and gone to heaven. That's just how beautiful it was. The sun had just begun to rise, the ocean was bluer than the sky, and the way the palm trees swayed through the tropical breeze had a mystic effect. From the airport, they took the team to a town called Texaco Village. When they arrived there, he soon learned what the British Commonwealth was. Trinidad was a colony of the Commonwealth. In other words, Trinidad belonged to England. The black natives that lived there were subordinates, just like it was during slavery times in the Americas, Australia, and South Africa.

There were two classes of servants. The setup was like this: they had house niggers and field niggers. The house niggers wore white coats and they cleaned and served for the white master, while the other natives worked the fields. When the British or Germans came into the Texaco Village, each one of them would have a servant.

During meal times in the cafeteria, each one of them would have a servant to go get them whatever they wanted. In fact, all of them had servants while they ate. John couldn't handle the fact that he had an older man, who could have been his father, serving him. He wanted the man to sit down and eat with him, not serve him! It disturbed him deeply. He got a chance to talk to the natives about their position as slaves, but many of them were afraid to have that discussion. It was as if the British had told them not to talk to the athletes about anything like that.

The next day the competition began. The team arrived at the stadium which to John's surprise was filled with black people. He had been in stadiums with large crowds, but the crowds there had been from many different ethnicities. There were white people from England and Germany, but this arena held ninety-nine percent black people. John was so impressed by what he saw: it gave him energy!

John created other activities when he was not in the competition. The name of the game for him was to get himself into that audience to meet and learn as much as he could about the people. He asked them many questions about their everyday life: if they had girlfriends or boyfriends, what kind of drinks were popular amongst the youth, did they attend school, and others. As a youngster John had drunk Old Thunderbird and Gypsy Rose, while in Trinidad the main drink was rum. After he learned about their activities, he found out that they were very much like him. He became friends with many of the people, and those who had young daughters introduced John to them.

John was in awe of the whole setting, except for the hot, humid climate. In terms of the climate, there was one thing that he could not understand: how the police could wear the clothes that they wore in such a hot climate. Their attire was for a cold climate like their homeland, England. They wore a mounted police hat, woolen shirt, woolen short pants, and long woolen socks. Everyone else, John said, was damn near in his or her birthday suit. There was something else that he found interesting, and that was the grass track that they had. John had seen a dirt track, clay, and tartan track. The only other grass track that he has seen since that time is the grass track at College of the Desert in Palm Desert, California.

The earth was so hot on the grass track that the wasps would build their homes there; and when the race began, they would fly up from the ground. John was not accustomed to that because in New York, when one saw a bumble bee or wasp, he or she would try to get out of the way. To the natives, however, it was a natural occurrence for them in their environment.

In his first international race John ran the one
hundred meters. He placed first, and he felt good about
what he had done. The people in the stands that he had
met were even more impressed. The medals that the
athletes had won were different, too. Instead of giving
the usual gold medal, they gave John a China Malone
clock. He said it was beautiful! He really loved that
clock. He spoke to me of that clock in a way that made
me think that it was more than silver or gold. Adolf
Plumber fell in love with the clock and he wanted one
desperately, so he told John to tell the officials that he
wanted to run the race again along with him. John did
what he asked, and Adolf asked if he could make a deal
with him. Adolf really put a psych job on John. He said,
"Tomorrow, in the race, there will not be any competition, except you and me. So, what we will do is both
of us will come out slow, and when we get to the ten
meter line, we will sprint it out." John agreed to do just
what Adolf had said, thinking that what he said was
valid. However, the next day, he found out that Adolf
had other motives.

When the race began the next day, John had
planned to keep his side of the deal. World record holder
Adolf was older then John, and John had a great respect
for him. When they lined up for the race, Adolf winked
at John and said, "Remember what I said." The officials
set them off with the gun, and Adolf broke out like a bat
out of hell while John came out lackadaisically. John
could not believe what he was seeing. He became upset
with Adolf after winning second place, but because of
the respect, he did not respond negatively. After the race,
Adolf received his clock. He had accomplished his goal.
He knew that he had lost John's respect, and he had to

bring John back to gain his regard for him by telling him that he had put a psyche job on him, so he walked up to John and said, "That was a psych job I put on you. You are going to be one of the greatest runners of all times. Don't you ever let anybody put a psych job on you." John understood clearly where Adolf was coming from. He learned from a master that to be the best in the game of track and field one had to have control of the mind, never allowing anyone to defeat you for any reasons other than your own.

Adolf and John hit it off real well. They would compete against each other again. Adolf was an excellent runner in several events, and he decided to run in the quarter mile race. John decided to run it, too. John was not used to running long distances at that time. He started out strong, leading the race due to his excellent speed, but speed was not enough. The race required endurance. He led the race for about three hundred yards, and after that, the top two runners in the race left him behind. He placed third.

The officials who issued the awards gave John a stainless silverware set, and the second place winner received a Papermate Pen. Adolf had won second place and John thought that they had made a mistake, so he gave Adolf the China set in exchange for the Papermate Pen. During that time, the Papermate Pen was popular in New York so he did not mind the exchange. Nevertheless, when the officials saw what John had done, they took the pen from him and returned the China. The people saw John's kind gesture, and they liked him even more. After the race that evening, he asked Skinner, the winner of the quarter mile race, why the officials had given him the China set. Skinner told John that the people wanted the visitors to have nice prizes to take home.

The people liked John very much, and they introduced him to their daughters, and he got involved with one of them, spending much time with her. Several of his teammates had girls too. John told the fellows on the team that when they went to breakfast or dinner that they should take their girls with them. Thinking this was a good idea, they agreed. The next morning, the fellows got their girls and took them to breakfast. They sat at the table and talked, hugged, and kissed on occasion, too. The servants served them as usual. They never said a word about them having the native girls there. They simply refused to serve them. They placed the guys' food on the table, and they kept right on serving everyone, except the native girls. John began to study the situation. He reflected back on the oppression of blacks in the States, and suddenly, it dawned on him how widespread this problem was. Black people were divided against one another in the States, Trinidad, and other places.

He got uptight about the situation, demanding that the servants serve the girls.

I want all of you who are serving to get one thing straight. We brought these girls here to have breakfast with us. We understand that you have been trained not to treat your own people as free men and women, but today is a new day! If you cannot serve these women that are with us, then do not serve us anything! I mean it! These are our guests, and they will be served or we will not eat here. Don't bring nothing else over here!

The servants looked at John, and they knew that he was serious. They seemed surprised at what John had said, and they obeyed his request to feed the native girls. They could not believe that he could be so adamant about such a thing.

Although the situation looked negative, the servants saw John as a hero and an activist. The word got around amongst the servants about what John had done in the cafeteria. They loved and respected him even more because he stood up for them. The result was that the native girls were served, and John became a symbol of hope for the Trinidadians.

Other individuals came over later to compete in Trinidad. There was Leon "Duma" Coleman, Otis Burrell, Jim Kemp, and Charles Green. John got to know them well on short notice, and like most young men do, they went out looking for girls. They met some models from the island, and the girls liked them so much that they felt comfortable going to a club with them. The club atmosphere was different from what John had been used to. It had a live band and the musicians were singing Calypso music.

There was much conversation and laughter while they drank and listened to the music. John loves music and for a moment he concentrated on the lyrics to a song that was being sung. He said that he was spellbound when he discovered that the musicians were singing about him. They were singing about his exploits and his future. John said that he thought about Manhattan Technical and Vocational High School where he won his first serious track meet. They had set a record in the mile relay and the cheerleaders at the other schools were so impressed that they created a song for him and his team. It was an honor for him to have had such an impact on the people that someone again would want to create a song about him.

Later on that evening, they had a Limbo contest. The music was grooving and John was feeling good. He said to someone, "I have to win this contest." So he got up and walked to the Limbo line and awaited his turn. When he got to the front to go under, the natives, the models, and his teammates cheered him on. He went back on his legs and got down low, and he walked under the Limbo stick. He went through three more rounds without knocking the stick off the holder. It came down to him and another guy from the island. John was psyched up, and the people cheering him made it all the more fun. He won the Limbo contest. John said that he did not know if the natives allowed him to win, but it felt good. It was a night that he will never forget.

The two-week track meet had come to a close, and it was time to return home. Pan Am airlines was experiencing financial problems, and it was decided by the workers that they would strike. The manager broke the news to the athletes that they could not leave the island because Pan Am was the only airline at that time to fly to Trinidad. No one knew exactly how long the strike would last, but it lasted 30 days.

John made the best of the situation, and he continued to train everyday. One day he was running on the beach and met a man who lived on an old wrecked ship. Although he looked like an Indian, he was a Trinidadian who rode a bicycle that had no tires. He was different from many of the other Islanders because he had his own ideas about the way things should be. He took a liking to John and he talked to him about his occupation as a fisherman. The man invited John to spend a day to fish with his friends. John thought that the men would fish about two hours and then have a fish fry, but it was quite the contrary. The fishermen fished all day long, pulling nets with thousands of fish in them. John couldn't go longer than two hours. It was best that he stick with track and field.

After a while, John wanted a drink. So the natives told him that they would make him a drink if he went up in the tree and got some coconuts. The coconut trees were grown in such a way that they would go out in a horizontal angle for so many feet and go up into a vertical. John walked along the horizontal part to begin to climb up vertical parts of it. It took him no longer that thirty minutes to climb to the top. When he got to the top, he reached up and knocked down several coconuts. Now it came time for him to come down, but no one told him the technique for getting down. The natives were trying to tell him to grab his hands around the tree and use his hands and feet simultaneously to bring himself down. He could not understand what they were saying, so he came down the best way he could. It took him an hour and a half to come down. John learned how to use the technique later when he saw the natives climb up a coconut tree. The natives were laughing at the man who could run so fast, but not climb trees. After he climbed down to the ground, the natives were pleased that he had not hurt himself. They took the coconuts, and made everyone some strong drinks using rum. John felt very comfortable being with them. They were so loving and warm, but when he talked about rebelling against the Colonial powers, there was tension in the air.

The thirty days in Trinidad were coming to a close, and John had gotten himself in trouble by getting involved with a woman of great beauty, charm, and grace. He said that if he had not been married, he would never have left that island. But the Pan Am strike was over, and he knew that he had to return to the states to reunite with his family. He exchanged numbers with several people and made sure that he gave his "temporary wife" his number too. On the day that they departed from Trinidad, he was sad that he had to leave, and happy because he was going to see his first wife Karen and his baby Kimmy.

When John returned to the states he saw a different side of Karen. She began to talk about what she wanted in their relationship. She knew what she desired from him as a husband and an athlete. She was prepared to be the backbone as he advanced in the athletic world. She had earned good grades in High School, and she was able to obtain a job easily. Karen became a legal secretary for a general in the military in Harlem, a big plus for their new family's financial situation. She also demanded that John keep a job to assist her with the finances. She believed in him so much that she began to build her life around him early in the marriage. He said that he told her not to do that because he was independent and needed space.

Before John had gone to Trinidad, he had had a job working at Lennox Hill Hospital. But he failed to contact his employer while in Trinidad, and discovered after he contacted them that he had been fired. The loss of job and having a new wife caused him some very serious problems in his house. Karen complained about the situation, and he needed to find work immediately in order to take care of his family.

In about a week's time he received a letter from Trinidad. He was in the shower when the letter arrived and Karen came into the bathroom with it. Being forgetful, he told her to open it. He was in the shower thinking about who might have written him so quickly. He got out of the shower, dried himself off, and got dressed. As he walked into the room where his wife was he saw this object coming at him and he moved just in time to keep it from hitting his head. John looked around to see what she had thrown: the China Malone clock that he had won in Trinidad. Karen was cussing and crying and at the same time asking him how he could be so cruel. The letter was from his sweetheart in Trinidad. She had written him expressing her love and admiration. She wrote about the special intimate times that they shared while he was there, and she was hoping that he would return soon.

John was young and immature and he definitely was wrong for what he had done, but he couldn't do anything except say that he was sorry and it would not happen again. John was very hurt that Karen had broken the clock, and he expressed that too. But Karen said, "I don't like the clock, nor what came with it. " So that was the end of that.

John's need for a job grew more desperate. He thought about all of the contacts that he had made, and he decided to ask the Puma company if they would give him a job. Prior to his going to Trinidad, Mr. Yance from the Pioneer Club had sent him over to the Puma company to receive some running shoes for his trip. The

Beconta company, a distributor for ski products and the Puma Shoe Company, was located at 440 Park Ave. South. When John picked up his shoes, he spoke to one of the owners whose name was James Woolner. Mr. Woolner became a mentor for John, and he was the gentleman that he spoke to when he returned from Trinidad seeking employment. Mr. Woolner was very receptive to John's situation, and he gave John a job working in the warehouse. The Puma company became his refuge; he could earn money to take care of his responsibilities while he continued to compete in track and field.

6

East Texas State University

Boy, Nigger, Nigra

John competed in New Jersey, and at this particular track meet there was a young man named Pete Peterson, a track and field scout from East Texas State University. Impressed by John's ability to run he introduced himself and the ETSU program. Pete spoke very highly of the school, saying that it was a nice place and everything would be fine if he chose to attend. When Pete returned he told the head track and field coach Delmer Brown about John and other athletes he had met. In a meeting over the phone Brown offered him a full scholarship, a job for his wife, and an opportunity for her to ride with the team on the bus to the track and field events. John had to consider his decision. He thought about how nice it would be to get his wife and child out of Harlem, and raise his daughter in a healthy environment. He decided to go and check out ETSU and see how things were, but his wife insisted that they go as a family.

John agreed and accepted the offer during the fall semester of the 1966-67 academic year. ETSU also offered a scholarship to Dennis Dice, a Jamaican friend of John's. John said that Dennis never felt that he was black; he always said that he was Jamaican, and that is all. They were supposed to be buddies, and he was telling John how they were going to be family, hanging out together and having a real good time in Texas. Dennis' and John's family left together on a plane heading to Texas, and when it arrived there, John got his first taste of brown-nosing and overt racism. They flew into Dallas, Texas, and track coach Delmar Brown met them there. Greeting

124

them with his strong southern accent, Coach Delmer felt compelled to explain Texas way of life when it comes to black folks. He began by showing them the bathroom for blacks and the one for whites. He talked about how the whites expect their Nigras to behave in their white society. He wanted them to know that things were done differently in Texas, and it was best they follow the status quo.

In about ten minutes during Coach Brown's talk, my new name became boy, Nigger, and Nigra. I had never heard of the word Nigra; it was a first for me. At any rate, I said to myself that I had made a mistake. Not so much for bringing myself into the situation, but my wife and child. It appeared that it was going to be a tragic situation. I was not accustomed to hearing boy, Nigger, Nigra, or anything else. I didn't have money at the time and I totally depended upon the scholarship. I certainly was not about to call my mother and father to bail me out. So I stuck it out.

During his first year, John discovered that ETSU had been integrated for just one year. It had been an all-white school, in a college town called Commerce. There were only a few track and field runners that were black. There were students such as: Jimmy Ray Smith, John Davis, Carl Richardson, Al Taylor, and Terry Barnett. John says that he and Terry had a lot of philosophical conversations. They also had a black kid named Sam Williams who played basketball. Jay Johnson, a former NFL player, was there too. There were also black athletes from the town that attended. He stated that the white Texans did not have a clue as to how to go about dealing with it. They were integrated by law, but not in their hearts and their minds. Why? Because one was still called a boy, Nigger, and treated as a second-class citizen.

John was not the studious type. He had, as mentioned earlier, dyslexia. On one occasion, he told coach Brown that he had some problems with his math class. Coach Brown said, "Don't worry, I will find someone to assist you." John said that coach Brown tried solving his problem by asking the team's trainer David to assist John with his math. David didn't know anything about math, and consequently John didn't do well in class. In fact, Coach Delmar Brown and his cronies made sure that athletes took courses that would keep them eligible for track and field. John took courses such as wrestling, tennis, recreation field work, tennis, golf, and the one class that Coach Brown taught, anatomy, who gave passing grades to all of the track and field athletes knowing that many of them did not pass the class academically. The coach and ETSU were not concerned about their education; they were only concerned about how they could build their track and field program to earn money for their programs and their pockets on side bets.

The first day that John hit the track was quite a memorable day for him. Coach Brown made a statement that if anyone could run under 28 seconds in the 300 yards, they didn't have to train that day. The coach had heard of John, but he had not seen him run. When John matriculated to ESTU he was in top physical condition, and when the coach made that statement, John made him eat his words. John ran it in 27.9 sec., and the coach was shocked. He was looking at his watch, smiling and grinning as if he had found a pot of gold. He said, "Boy, look at my horse run." John's name became "Horse" after his first run. He didn't like what he had called him so John expressed to coach Brown that his name was not Nigger, Nigra, boy, or horse; his name was John Carlos. The coach could see right from that point that John was not like the rest of the crew.

Further, John told him, "I am from Harlem, New York, not Texas, Mississippi, Alabama, or any other place, and I will tell you exactly where to get on and off when you address me any other way than as a man." Coach Brown played things off for a while, and called John by his name. After a while John accepted the name Horse, and he tried to maintain his integrity by not getting riled up when the coach would use the ugly names that were mentioned earlier.

Coach Brown was impressed with John's performance, and he was the number one man. Once John proved that he was the best, he reminded the coach that he had promised his wife a job. John explained to him that if he didn't get her a job that they were going to leave the following week. After seeing John run that 27.9 sec., he got Karen a job quickly, working for W. J. Bell, the mayor of the town, who was also the chairman of the journalism department at ETSU. Incidentally, John said that Coach Brown promised him several things after he arrived there. He promised to arrange tutoring for him, pay his medical bills, and he also stated that John would receive a monthly check for expenses. When none of these things materialized, John and his family were disappointed.

The blacks that lived there accepted racism because it was the norm. They also allowed the whites to keep them from prospering. Their dreams were crushed; they were depressed and suppressed at the same time. John dealt with it by speaking openly to blacks about how to combat the racists. He did not back down from any kind of racist remarks. He told everyone who crossed him with racist remarks where to get on and off. Further, he told the blacks that lived there, "You do not have to take the shit that is going down if you stick together."

John's daughter Kimmy got a dose of the racist medicine too. One day while playing with other white children, she ran into the house crying, not from being physically hurt, but from being injured by her neighbor's racist remarks when he screamed at her. He had no understanding or compassion for the two-year-old child. John went outside and told the man that his daughter was a child, only two years old. He said, "You better not ever speak to her in any kind of negative way." John told him that if he had anything to say, he damn sure better say it to him and not his daughter. John got things straight with him, and the man understood where he was coming from. The situation tried his nerves, but God kept him from bashing someone for hurting his baby's feelings.

Time seemed to move at a snail's pace while John was trying to adapt to this new and sometimes hostile environment. He got first-hand experience with some of the things that he had heard from the blacks in Harlem that were from the South. He saw a cotton gin, cotton fields, and people picking cotton. It was a hell of a contrast from the Cotton Club in Harlem where the prettiest women and the handsomest men in the world danced and sang in front of white folks for a living. What a difference in cotton!

The track and field season began in January. East Texas State University and the colleges and universities on the east coast of the US had different climates. The indoor season was in progress on the East coast while the outdoor season was in progress in the West. ETSU was in the Lone Star Conference when John set a national record during his freshman year, 1965-66. He ran 9.2 seconds in the 100-yard dash, and 20.02 seconds in the 220-yard dash. This was in the early part of the track season. The Lone Star Conference consisted of Prairie View College, Texas Southern University, East Texas State University, Texas A&M, South West Texas State University, Sam Houston University, Steven F. Austin, Howard Payne, and McMurry College. Many of the meets were held in small towns in Texas, and there was no major recognition for John who was running at world record times. So John wrote letters to the track and field promoters in New York, Boston, Canada, Washington DC, Los Angeles, Philadelphia, and other places to obtain recognition for ETSU. The major competition never came to Texas, they invited John to compete at meets, but didn't accept anyone else from his team. When Coach Brown got word that John had sent letters to the promoters he became "pissed off." But that was the only way John was going to be able to compete against the best in the country. Coach Brown's anger did not move John at all.

The state of Texas had never heard of anyone at that time running as fast as John did. Many people were asking themselves, "Who is this guy named Carlos?

Could there be a Mexican running that fast?" The name Carlos caused many to wonder about John's ethnicity.

The team traveled from school to school in station wagons. There were many occasions that they had to change clothes in the car before an event. The fields were their bathrooms because the Jim Crow customs were adhered to by whites and blacks. Blacks had their facilities and whites had theirs. Because Coach Brown was trained in the customs of the racists' ways he wanted the black athletes to wait in the car and eat while the whites ate in the restaurant. John refused to accept that "bullshit," and he told the coach that he would not tolerate that kind of behavior. Either they all ate together or they didn't eat at all.

John and the coach had another disagreement, which came about when he overheard him talking to another coach, telling him that his Niggers could outrun the other team. So Coach Brown and the other coach made a bet on their Niggers. John didn't like what he had heard, and when they got to the track meet he told the coach that he didn't want to run the mile relay. The coach didn't know that he had overheard him make a bet on that race. John told him that they had enough fast people to win. The coach was so pissed off, John said, "And he told me that I didn't have to run at all." He knew that this particular track meet was not important, so that is why he didn't allow John to run.

At the Austin Relays track and field event, John didn't have to run. So he and the school reporter, and photographer, went to a bar in the city of Austin, Texas. The two men that he was with were white. They walked into the bar together and ordered beer. The bartender was a white guy, and he brought over two beers. John asked him politely where his beer was, and his response was that he didn't sell beer to Niggers. John told him that he didn't want to buy a Nigger, he wanted to buy a beer. The bartender repeated the racial remarks, and John became angry because he had had enough "racial bullshit." So he reached over and grabbed the bartender and pulled him over the counter. He did it so quickly that the bartender didn't have time to think what was happening to him. He was surprised and he knew that he could not defeat John in hand-to-hand combat. John was prepared to kick this dude's ass all over the bar, but he ran into a problem. By using his peripheral vision, he saw two Mexicans who were playing pool run at him with their sticks, ready to defend the bartender. John was too quick for that shit and he turned the bartender loose and backed himself to the door. He forgot about the bartender, and he concentrated on the two Mexican guys and became more angry because they had tried to help the white guy.

John looked at them and asked them what their problem was. They said nothing. He was sure that they heard the bartender call him a Nigger. Then he said, "Why would you help the very people who came here from Europe and took your land?" He got no response. They made it out of there without having to hurt anyone or being themselves hurt. John said to himself, "Not only am I running for ETSU, but I am running for the state of Texas, and I can't even buy a beer because my skin is the wrong color in the white Texan's eye." Although he was in a white racist area, he refused to give in to them under any circumstances.

On the one hand, John was the coach's bread and butter, and on the other, he was a thorn in his side. You see, the more John would win, the more recognition the coach would receive, and the more money the college would receive. This is the one thing that many college athletes, their parents, and fans don't understand. The athletes are earning the colleges, universities, coaches, NCAA, scouts, television, newspapers, and magazines, a host of riches, while the athletes have to beg for the crumbs off the table because the NCAA says that they are operating in an amateur status.

John needed money. He had a wife and child to take care of. So, he went to the coach like a man and asked him to assist him in obtaining a job. John had to sit there and watch Coach Brown ponder to see if he was a good enough boy to get one. But John being his bread and butter, he put him in the category of a good boy. John got a job and purchased a Ford Mustang. This gave him the privilege of driving himself around, avoiding racist confrontation.

ETSU had an excellent regular track and field season. It was a sure thing that they were going to compete in the state conference, where John placed ETSU on the map with a national record of 9.2 in the 100 yd. dash. He had other great record times, running 9.4 sec. in the 100 yd. dash at North Eastern University. He ran a 19.7 in the 220 yd. dash, and 3.21 in the mile relay.

Willie Turner from the University of Oregon was considered the world's fastest freshman after he tied John's 9.2 sec. record in the 100 yd. dash. Willie received this kind of acclaim because he attended a PAC 8 school that had name recognition. He led the nation as a freshman in the 100 yd. dash, running a 9.2, and in the 200 yd. dash he ran 20.2.

The football team was doing well also. So well that ETSU decided to purchase for the football team some very expensive championship rings. Upon seeing this, John felt that if the football team received rings for being champions, the track team should receive rings also. It wasn't until they had an all-team meeting when John decided to tell the coaching staff that he wanted to have a ring like the football team. Prior to John venting his feelings about the rings, the coach mentioned the fact that they were going to receive some kind of skimpy award if they won the state championship. John raised his hand and told the coach that he did not want the award; he told him that he wanted the same thing that the football team received. The coach said in a derogatory manner, "Why can't you Nigras be satisfied." John responded by saying, "If you want to win the state conference, you better provide the rings." Looking at John with disgust, the coach knew that he meant business. John had proven that he had the ability to defeat their opponents. He was their sure winning ticket to the championship, and Coach Brown reluctantly agreed to provide the rings upon their winning.

Now the state conference was one day away. The team had been traveling and working hard with their routine workouts, and for some reason the coach somehow got a little on the ridiculous side. The coach asked them to run a step down which consists of a two hundred twenty, a hundred meter, and some other things. He and John knew that if everyone ran the step down, it could possibly drain them for the conference. That day the football team was working out and there was a group of guys building a platform for the graduating class. John was really upset about having to run, but he attempted to do it. Coach Brown lined them up, and he blew the whistle. John began to run on the track at full speed as if he were running the real thing and when he hit the corner of the track, he slowed down to a jog into a walk. John walked about one hundred and fifty yards to the finish place. Angry as hell, the coach turned as red as a tomato, calling John a Nigger and all kinds of things. Many people witnessed the coach's racist remarks.

After John heard the coach call him a Nigger, he took off all of his clothes until he was naked. He threw the clothes in the coach's face, and he went into the locker room to take his name off the locker and gather his equipment. He took his gear to the storage room and quit. After he did that, he started to take his last shower. Coach Brown came to him in the shower trying to apologize. John told the coach that he had better get out of his face because he was about to hurt him something fierce. He left the showers, got dressed, and began walking to his house. With his son Danny, Coach Brown approached John with a hammer in his hand, and John looked at him and told him that if he came at him with that hammer he better think of it as licorice because he would make him eat it. John added, "Old man, it is best that you give that hammer to your son and let him take this ass whipping." John walked back into the locker room and Coach Brown apologized to him again. He refused to accept it. So the coach left!

The news spread like wildfire that John was going to leave Texas. The car dealership contacted him, saying that he could not leave the state with the car, and John being young and not knowing much, didn't leave. Prior to this incident, things had been getting nastier, and he had decided to send his wife and child back home. His wife asked him what the problem was and he explained to her that he might have to hurt someone and he did not want to get his family involved. She understood where he was coming from, but she was reluctant to leave. But she eventually agreed and began to pack for her departure. John was relieved when she left.

In the meantime, the coaches and track athletes held a meeting to try and determine how to persuade John to return and run for the conference championship. They got their game plan together, and later on that day, John was approached by the coaches and athletes. They asked if they could talk to him about the situation. John told them that they could talk to him only if the players that he was with could come along. They agreed! They all walked over to the cafeteria. Food was provided to all of the participants in the room. The coaches began with an apology from Coach Brown; the players sobbed over the fact that they could not win without him. They also reminded him about the rings. The apology ceremony had an effect on John and he thought about the situation carefully. In about thirty minutes he agreed to run. However, he told them that after he ran in the conference, he was not going to run for ETSU anymore.

Many of the students heard that John was leaving and they decided to throw him a going away party. When he encountered his friends, he told them that he had changed his mind to continue to run, but would be leaving after the state conference. They were elated and they threw him a party. Anyway the party began as soon as the sun went down.

I couldn't say how long we were into the party, but after a while, the Junior Klan arrived in their super fast sports cars. There were about eight or ten cars there. They got out of their cars shouting racial slurs. They called us Niggers, apes, coons, and all kinds of ungodly things. Everyone in the party was checking them while they were talking trash. Then a couple of them took their shotguns out and they shot the windows out. Everyone hit the floor. Luckily, no one got hit. Me and my partners got our shotguns out and waited. The Klan didn't know that we had guns too. So when they finished shooting and got back into the car, me and a couple of my friends stepped outside the door and blew the back window out on a couple of their cars.

The Jr. Klan left there in a hurry. The party participants cleaned up the glass and continued with the party. They never heard from the Klan again.

The next day, the team piled into station wagons and cars and went to the state conference. It was a major event, and John was the star of the day. He defeated everyone in the 100 yd. dash, running 9.5. In the 220 yd. dash he ran 19.7, and in the mile relay the team ran 3.21. He earned enough points single- handily to win the state championship. Coach Brown was a happy soul. The entire team was joyful, and in time they received their rings.

Even though John had won the state championship, he was unhappy. His struggles with the coach, Jim Crow, and blacks that would not stand up against the racist whites had gotten the best of him. He stood alone!

He didn't like the words Nigra, boy, or Nigger. He gave respect as a man, and he demanded to be treated like a man. Everywhere he went, he would not allow anyone to treat him as anything less than a man.

At this time, a possible Olympic boycott was in question and John was an Olympic prospect. Consequently, people were asking questions about his views. ETSU's school reporter came to John and asked if he would be willing to do an article on racism on the campus and the Olympic Boycott. This was kind of a surprise to John: that someone would ask him to do this kind of interview. John found out (through a phone call from his wife) that the reporter had met her before she left. She had given him information about John, and she assured him that John would be receptive to an interview. John agreed to do the interview under one condition: that the reporter quote him word for word. The reporter agreed, and they began to do the interview. John talked about his experiences with the administration, the faculty, the coaches at ETSU, and the community. He revealed all of the negative things that he had experienced. He told the reporter about the name calling, the Junior Klan, Jim Crow customs, the coach's attitude, and the racist comments from whites in the community. As far as the Olympics were concerned, he believed that blacks should boycott the games because of America's ill treatment of blacks in this country. The reporter was true to his word and he quoted him word for word. He bypassed the standard procedure, and copied the article without the approval of his superiors. This article created a nightmare for ETSU and the reporter.

When the school paper came out there was an uproar on campus. ETSU was not pleased with John

Carlos' antics and they were especially angry with the white reporter who dared to write verbatim what John had to say about racism and the Olympics. The article was sent to other universities and colleges in Texas because the schools exchange newspaper stories with each other. ETSU was so angry at the reporter that they wanted to kick him out of school. John felt really bad for him, and at the same time he applauded him for his courage in writing this article. From this one article, many newspapers across the state of Texas came to John asking for interviews.

Shortly after this, John received a call to do an interview for *The Dallas Times*. He not only got a chance to talk about racism in Texas and the United States of America. He also stated poignantly that African-Americans should boycott the 1968 Olympics.

> African-Americans helped to build this country with free labor; they have built athletic programs that generate millions and now billions of dollars. The NCAA and the Olympic Committee collect this money and they establish business empires that generate jobs from CEO executives to janitors. They are scrutinized by their own people meaning that they are a tax free entity. And in their empire building, they seldom embrace the ones who work and sweat on playgrounds, fields, abandoned lots, and ghetto streets perfecting skills that people from every walk of life will come and pay to see. The Olympic committees do not have to answer to anyone. So who's to say who's putting their hands in the pot to take money illegally and

make crooked deals? The truth will be revealed one day!

The colleges and universities do the same thing. They build large arenas from the revenues that they make from ticket sales and hire coaches, scouts, and a host of other individuals to keep the new slave trade in athletics going in order to fill their pockets with money that should be shared with those who help to make it. Some of the coaches earn six digits, while the universities collect millions of dollars from ticket sales, food and beverages, play-offs, commercials, TV rights, paraphernalia, and booster clubs. The only thing that the athlete receives is a scholarship and/or a worthless medal. Now some of you will say, "What about athletes who go to the professional ranks?" Let's look into that.

According to the article "The Moat," by Steve Rushin, the NCAA governs 925 colleges and universities totaling around 300,000 athletes across the United States. How many jobs are there in professional baseball, basketball, football, and other sports? It is a ball park figure of about 2,500 jobs. That is not even ten percent of the athletes that the NCAA governs. What about the other 297,500 students who won't receive a million dollar contract from the pros? Many of them are chasing a dream that is only open to the chosen few who have the ability to compete at the highest levels. In other words, many of these athletes fall by the wayside, never reaching their potential, all because the colleges and institutions dangle a carrot in their face with a dream that often turns into a nightmare.

There are several white Olympic athletes that have the same problem. They have won medals and have not received any monetary compensation for their success. They are probably wondering why the Olympic Committee chose other individuals and placed them next to God such as a Bruce Jenner, Peggy Fleming, and Bill Tomey. The Olympic Committee embraced them, giving them opportunity to earn millions for the Olympics and earn riches for themselves while others earned little or nothing. Mark Spitz, a seven gold medal winner, was the only Super Star who did not allow the Olympic Committee to mold him into a puppet. Mark Spitzs declared that he would be his own man and I respect him for his decision to be a man.

The article from the *Dallas Times* came to the attention of the ETSU's Athletic Director, Jesse Harthorn, a racist and a member of the Olympic Committee. He called a meeting for all the black athletes. John said Jesse Harthorn came into the room, with his ego, specifically stating, "If any of you Niggers don't like it here, you can leave!" He asked if anyone had any questions, and John raised his hand. Mr. Harthorn never responded. He never allowed him to speak because he figured that someone would pick up on what he was saying. He asked if anyone wanted to leave. John raised his hand and said that he wanted to leave. When none of the other athletes said a thing John was truly disappointed. The meeting ended and again the white man had stood his ground over the fact that he could treat blacks any kind of way and they would accept it. John Carlos again stood alone!

John discovered later why the black athletes didn't speak when they had the opportunity. At that time, the Vietnam War and the draft were going on, and those individuals who were not in a college or university would be drafted immediately. So if they had chosen to leave school, the government would have drafted them during the transition from one school to another. John didn't have to worry about that situation because he was married with a child. But he says he would have spoken against the athletic director even if he hadn't been married.

During this time of protest, John saw that his message to the black athletes was not successful. So he began to talk to the blacks on campus. He told them that it was time to speak out. He told them that every major newspaper in the country would be focused on them because he had been interviewed for several articles on racism and discrimination at ETSU and in America. The slave mentality of the blacks in Texas was based on many years of servitude, and John had hoped that he could liberate some of the frustrations by giving them a voice. But they refused to respond! John stood seemingly alone in the struggle with the exception of the young white reporter who stuck his neck out to expose the racism in Texas and in America. John wished that he could have helped him in his struggle with the school authorities, but when you fight for freedom, justice, and equality, sometimes you have to face things alone. This was a trying time for John because after the meeting and all, he began to receive hate letters and death threats from all over the country.

John was at a crossroads, and socially he struggled, due to the fact that the authorities never did anything with blacks in mind. Everything that the system did was geared towards the Anglo-Saxon male. John did not see any black instructors, nor did he see anyone in his books that looked like him. He was surrounded by people who were programmed to accept anything that the whites would hand down. He had no role models to follow! The business community was lily white. The government officials, police, doctors, dentists, lawyers, and every phase of economic goodness was white. Thus, John had to respond to this whiteness with the blackness that God had given him by speaking out against the bigotry that was perpetrated against the black man. Ultimately, he left ETSU and returned to Harlem.

After returning to Harlem, John received a call from Harry Edwards, an Associate Professor of Sociology at San Jose State University about a possible boycott of the 1968 Olympics. Harry was the head spokesman for the boycott, and he was trying to bring some key figures to the table for debate. A sketch of Harry's life will help to explain how he got himself involved with the black movement at the national level. Harry was raised in the ghetto of the South end of East St. Louis, in a situation that is persistent in any ghetto. There is poor housing, little or no education, shortage of jobs, large families, family separation, rats, roaches, and constant chaos. It is a place where children grow up very quickly, having to fend for themselves. There is little or no adult supervision, and anything that one can get into goes. One can get into drugs, crime, sex, alcohol, pornography, numbers running, pimping and hustling in a fast lane that leads to jail, prison, depression, insanity, spiritual death, disease, drug addiction, and eventually death. Harry and several of his brothers got caught up in the system, and several of them went to prison due to this nasty environment.

Harry attended Junior High School and High School in St. Louis where he played sports. He was blessed to have tremendous height, standing six feet eight inches tall. He played basketball and track. Doing well in both sports, he earned an athletic scholarship to San Jose State University in 1960. He attended SJSU because of the great reputation of black athletes that attended school there. The scouts that recruited him told him that everything would be great if he attended their school. But to the contrary, he never realized in his wildest dreams that he would encounter racism at the level that he did at school. At that time the student population at SJSU was growing rapidly, but there were only around 100 to 200 blacks on a campus of about 20,000 students. So blacks were the minority and they were discriminated against in housing, student services, fraternities, sororities, and everything else. Additionally, the majority of black athletes that were recruited by SJSU were advised to take physical education courses. They were seldom pushed towards other academic disciplines. But Harry had his own mind, and he got serious about his education, graduating from SJSU with a degree. Further, he earned a master's degree from Cornell University, and after some years of teaching he earned a doctoral degree in sociology from UC Berkeley.

Subsequent to being hired by SJSU in 1966, Harry made a name for himself. After teaching for a couple of semesters, Harry realized that the same game of discrimination and racism was being played during his stay at SJSU. So one day he got together with a friend who was a former student athlete named Ken Noels. They had discussions about the activities, and they determined that racism in the fraternities, sororities, housing, and the lack of understanding of the administration was still a serious problem. So they began to gather evidence of discrimination, and after they established their case, they made arrangements to present it to the administration. They were referred to the Dean of Students, Stanley C. Benz. They presented their case, and Dean Benz literally laughed in their face, making it perfectly clear that the whites were not interested in racial equality. So Harry and Ken went to the local press.

When newspaper released the story, the administration got wind of it. They were forced to deal with the issues which had become public. Also the school was largely dependent on state and federal funds, and there had been laws on the books that forbade discrimination based on sex, race, and religion. The administration was forced to change their policy or they would loose federal and state funds. The president of SJSU allowed his vice president to conduct hearings which meetings lasted three days, and all those who had an issue could speak. The hearings were very successful, and Harry established a national reputation from that event because the story went national. Harry and Ken did an excellent job exposing racial discrimination at SJSU.

The phone call that John received from Harry was to inform him that Dr. Martin L. King Jr. had made a specific request to meet him at a meeting that had been scheduled to discuss the Olympic Boycott. John was honored, for he had much love and admiration for Dr. King and he was very anxious to meet him, so he agreed to attend. The phone call ended with some talk about John possibly matriculating to San Jose State University.

While attending ETSU, John subscribed to *Track and Field.* One day he walked into the mailroom to pick up his mail, and in the issue there was an article on San Jose State University's track team. The magazine reported how Tommy Smith, Lee Evans and others were breaking national and world records in the relays and sprints from the quarter mile down to the 50 yd. dash. John was impressed with what he read. He thought SJSU's track and field runners were the new revolution in track and field and he knew he could defeat them all if he had an opportunity. It was from that occurrence in the mailroom that he became interested in transferring to SJSU.

He got his chance to visit that same year when he was invited to compete in the Amateur Athletic Union (AAU) Nationals in San Diego at Balboa Stadium. He and George Anderson, a runner from Southern University, were good friends and they decided to visit SJSU after the AAU meet was over. During that visit, he and George got a chance to meet Tommy Smith, SJSU's Coach Bud Winters, and Art Simburg. John did not meet Harry Edwards during that visit, but he went by his office while touring the campus. At that moment John couldn't know that each of these men would play an important part in his life.

Harry's reason for the meeting was to promote his program called The Olympic Project for Human Rights. It was his intention to get Dr. King's support. John was informed late about the meeting. On the day of the meeting he got caught up in something, and he arrived there a few minutes late at the hotel across the street from Madison Square Garden. There were some very distinguished guests there: Dr. Martin Luther King Jr., Andrew Young, and Ralph Abernathy. When John entered the room the meeting had just begun. Harry introduced John to everyone, and the meeting continued. Harry spoke about his plans to boycott the 1968 Olympics. He stated poignantly that he wanted to expose racism and the oppression of black people in America to the world. He wanted to accomplish this task in a nonviolent way, and he knew that this concept would be appealing to Dr. King. After Harry spoke, Dr. King talked to them about his position on the boycott. John said that when Dr. King spoke, he was in total awe!

Then the floor was opened for discussion. John asked Dr. King why he was interested in this challenge. Dr. King mentioned that there were other black organizations such as SNCC, the black Panthers, Muslims, and other organizations that were not committed to the nonviolent way of protesting. He went on to say that the Olympic Boycott was a nonviolent protest, and it coincided with what his philosophy was all about. He was tired of having his followers beaten by police, bitten by dogs, spit on, knocked down with powerful fire hoses, and hit by rocks and bottles. He said that the boycott could reach its goal without violence.

He gave illustrations about the man on whom he patterned his nonviolent philosophy: Mahatma Gandhi. Everyone listened attentively to Dr. King, and John said that he was set on fire inside just to have been in the same room with him, that he would have done anything for him.

Finally, Dr. King said to them, "I would like to go with you to the Olympics to boycott, if I return from Memphis, Tennessee." That statement stopped John in his tracks. John asked him in a very serious way, "What do you mean, if you return from Memphis?" Dr. King explained to the committee that someone had threatened his life by a letter and a phone call saying that there was a bullet with his name on it, and he did not have to wait long to get it. John asked him if he was going to go to Tennessee. Dr. King said that he was committed to the cause of the people in Tennessee, and he believed that the people who threatened his life were serious about killing him. He continued to speak about the situation, ready to face the opposition with boldness and courage. Showing no fear at all he stated boldly, "Yes, I am going to Memphis!" John gathered strength from Dr. King, and he knew that he was at that meeting for a purpose. Dr. King was a man for whom John had the utmost respect. They were dealing with the United States Government, and Dr. King gave him the reinforcement that he was doing the right thing by participating in the boycott. What a monumental task for a 23 year old!

I asked John how he handled his own death threats:

I am not afraid of them; I'm just John Carlos. My father and my Uncle Solomon fought for the rights and freedom of all Americans, and many black people died for that cause. I got strength from that. My manhood had been challenged by gangs, Irish cops, blacks from other neighborhoods, and many elements of white society. I am not afraid to die! I'm not afraid to kill! There is a time and place to do everything under the sun. Every one who sent me hate letters and death threats were cowards. They were cowards because they were not man or woman enough to send their return address in order to give me a chance to respond. I'm not a violent man! I was not going to go to each of their homes and confront them in any kind of way.

I would have drafted a letter explaining my position as a black man in America. I would have explained to them that no one is born a racist; hate is taught just like love is taught. Although I was not afraid, I was concerned about my family, and I had to conceal the threats. I responded differently to each one, but there was one threat that did cause some concern for me. This man from the South sent me a letter saying, "Dear Nigger, I don't like nothing about you nor your coon friends that are making trouble for this country. I am going to make this letter short and brief. Nigger, I am going to kill you and your entire family with the exception of your coon father. I'm going to rape him first, then I'm going to kill him. Signed, White Power!" The rape part really put the icing on the cake. Then I thought about where this guy's mind was. He resented the fact that my father was a man with intelligence, integrity, culture, and boldness and that instilled strength in me. He felt that if he could have sex with my father that he could somehow take away that manhood. He was probably a man who had been incarcerated in prison and enjoyed having sex with men. He was a sick man with a deranged mind, and I wish that he had sent his return address because he would have gotten his chance to deal with me in person.

At first, John could not understand why a man would want to kill another man because he stood up for freedom, justice, and equality. He said that Dr. King was not the kind of man who threatened anyone with bombs, knives, guns, or anything that caused violence like other black activists. He said that Malcolm X, on the other hand, had created a fear in the whites that shocked the very core of the pecking order: Malcolm did not mind telling the white man that he would use any means necessary to get where he was going. But Dr. King was quite the contrary.

John said that he has a strong love for both King and Malcolm and he feels they were good for each other in a sense because the whites had to decide whom they wanted to deal with. John strongly believes that many people promoted Dr. King because of Malcolm X. But after Dr. King told him about the death threats, and the assassination happened, John thought about it very deeply. He came to the conclusion that the white racists didn't kill Dr. King for his strong protest; he was killed because he got himself involved in the financial and economic game of American business. John thought even further and discovered that when the yellow, red, brown, and/or the black people talked to their own people about the economic destruction they faced, the whites would see that those people or individuals were killed, jailed or bought off immediately.

The abolitionist named John Brown came up in the conversation. He was called the true white man who believed in truth, justice, and equality for all men. As John put it, "He gave his life for what he believed, and when I go to heaven and see him, I will put my arms around him and call him friend and brother." John understands what causes a man to kill another man, for the love of money is the root of all evil.

Concerned about whether or not John was going to return, Coach Brown had contacted John while he was back in New York. John decided to return. While waiting for school to begin, he hung out in New York and was continuing to train for track until he decided to visit SJSU for a second evaluation of it. His evaluation would prove to be positive, but he did not know how to make the transition. By design, he ran into Art Simburg again. Art was the man who helped to recruit all of the great runners at SJSU. He was a short, portly guy who was clumsy at everything, except putting athletes together. Art was a track and field junkie, and he gravitated to John like a duck to water. They engaged in conversations about what they wanted to do in life, and John communicated to Art that he had to return to ETSU. Art decided to tag along with John because he felt that he could assist John with his track career. So when the time came, John and Art set off on a Greyhound bus for Commerce, Texas.

During the ride, they had lengthy discussions, exchanging stories about their lives, dreams, and ambitions. Art mentioned that he wanted to build the best track and field team in the world. It was kind of amusing to John to hear that Art was so interested in track and field, because Art was so clumsy. On the other hand, John discussed the problems he had with racism, and Art responded by saying that John should not have to deal with that kind of treatment.

They arrived in Commerce early in the morning, took a cab to the dorm where John lived, and got some rest. Later on that day, John met with Coach Brown and told him that he was interested in transferring to SJSU. Almost immediately, Coach Brown became angry and he began to accuse San Jose State of illegal recruiting practices. San Jose State had not talked to John about anything, but he could taste SJSU after having the long talk with Art. The coach threatened John something fierce, and that is what made him make the decision to leave ETSU for good.

John then returned to SJSU with Art, who gave him the breakdown as to how the track and field program worked. There were two basic operations for runners. They could run for the school or they could run for the Catholic Organization called the Santa Clara Youth Village (SCYV). The Youth Village had a building in the city of Santa Clara. Coach Bud Winters was the head track and field coach for SJSU, and Woody Lynn was the manager for SCYV. The Youth Village provided a way for these runners who were waiting to become eligible to compete at various colleges and universities across the United States and the world. Art took John to Jerry William's apartment to meet the other top track and field runners. Jerry was a top sprinter from Berkeley High School. He had sat out for a year or two, and he was making a comeback at the sport. He was mature, and well respected by all. Because of this, his apartment was the check-in place for all newcomers.

When Art knocked on the door, one of the runners answered it. They were permitted to come in, the introductions began and John got a chance to check the fellows out in the apartment. He said, "I had no desire to remain in that apartment because everyone there looked like a country boy wearing suspenders and taps on their tennis shoes. They were so countrified and different from the fellows that I had been accustomed to being around that I had to think real quick about remaining there." After a few introductions, John got a chance to meet Jerry. They bonded very quickly, becoming close friends. Right away, Jerry assisted John with finding a job at Lockheed where he worked on the assembly line. John also found a place to live renting a large yellow and brown house on 10th and Reed near Jerry Williams.

Jerry Williams and his wife Ethel (Pooche) became like brother and sister to John and his wife. Kimmy loved them too. They were a surrogate uncle and aunt to her. John wasn't earning much money at the time, and the Williams assisted his family with things that a family might need.

After getting his family situation together, John registered for a recreation class during the 1969 spring semester. He took a course in order to get himself into SJSU's system, and work towards certification to become a Recreation Supervisor for businesses, hospitals, corporations, etc. The instructor was an Asian man who got to know John fairly well. The class required each student to do a research paper, and John got one of his lady friends to do it for him. When he turned the report in to his instructor, the instructor said, "John, you did not write this paper." John admitted that he didn't, and the instructor still accepted it.

San Jose State University was known to the world as "Speed City." The Santa Clara Youth Village was an affiliate to SJSU. There were ten guys on the Speed City team that could run 9.3 seconds in the hundred-yard dash at any one time. They had so many great sprinters that they had to break the team up into small groups, sending them to different track meets in order to give everyone a chance to compete. Further, the Speed City team was ranked number one in the world, and that is a feat in itself. John wanted to give recognition to the brothers who ran with him on the Speed City team: Dr. Kirk Clayton, Jerry Williams, Sam Davies, Bill Gaines, Lee Evans, Bob Griffin, Frank Slaton, Prof. Tommy Smith, Ronnie Ray Smith and John Carlos.

John predicted a national championship in track and field, and others predicted that they would break the world's record in the 440 relays, 100 yd. dash, 880, 200-meter, and without question the mile relay. The entire track and field world was looking at them. But UCLA, USC, and other powerhouse schools refused to run against them during the regular track season.

While waiting to become eligible, he worked and ran for the Santa Clara Youth Village---Speed City. They were invited to run at various colleges and universities around the world in the open events. The competition brought a great interest to the area, and people paid to watch them run. As a matter of fact, they ran so well that the owner and operators of the events were able to finance other sports programs from the revenues.

John thought that Speed City began with them in the 1967-68 school year. He did not realize its history until he received a letter from a young graduate student and sports historian named Urla Hill from SJSU. The letter contained some very important information about the history of Speed City that began in the 1950s with Ray Norton and Bob Poynter. These two men were the ones who put the late coach Bud Winter's SJSU track and field team on the map. According to Ms. Hill, the Speed City era had three distinct periods from 1956 to 1969.

SJSU's Speed City Team was the first track and field program to have a tartan track. The 3-M Company provided it. As a matter of fact, the track was the first eight-lane all-weather track in the world. It was one of the most innovative advancements in track and field for the most spectacular group of track and field men ever to assemble in one place. And what is so ironic about setting up the track for an all-black team was the fact that when the 3-M Company began to market the tartan track, they chose to use an all-white cast.

> I told the people at the 3-M company point blank that if there were no blacks in the commercials, two things would occur. The first thing that would happen is that the team would not endorse the track. Secondly I went on to tell them that if no blacks were in the commercial, we would tear the track up and make them get the hell out of our school. They knew that I meant business, and they agreed to hire blacks and place them in the commercial. The 3-M company really had nerve to come into our school and disrespect us like that. But I put their asses in check real quick! They got what they wanted and we got ours.

John's new coach at SJSU was named Bud Winters. John said that he was a great individual as a person and a coach. Bud had a lot on the ball when it came to coaching. For example, John's form was very unorthodox. He ran rather wild, but when Bud got him to learn the proper techniques for running, his style was like watching poetry in motion. Now he ran effortlessly. Coach Bud and John were made for each other!

> The most important thing that I learned from Coach Bud was the mental part of the game. Having the will to win and conditioning one's self to run under any climactic conditions requires a strong mind that is disciplined to the core.

John had much admiration and appreciation for Coach Bud. He thought about the situation that Coach Bud was in, in terms of having a lot of top athletes like Tommy Smith, Lee Evans, Ray Norton and other greats, but not having won an NCAA Championship. Feeling that he deserved that honor, John told Bud that he was going to make sure that he got his chance to win it. John told him that he would run for him for one year during the 1968-69 academic year, and he predicted he would win him an NCAA National Championship that Tommy Smith, Lee Evans, and Ray Norton hadn't produced.

7

1968 Olympics, Mexico City

Controversy

There was much controversy as to why the International Olympic Committee chose to have the 1968 Olympics in Mexico City. There was the high altitude that plagued most athletes. Then there were the student protests, riots, and shootings in the streets of Mexico City. The water and food from Mexico could cause people to become very sick with diarrhea. The stadiums and accommodations were not ready to host the large number of people that the International Olympic Committee had anticipated attending the event. And for the first time in the history of the Games, the athletes would use a synthetic or tartan track. Puma and Adidas were experimenting with a new type of shoe for the tartan track. Puma had a shoe called the Brush Shoe, which had 68 tiny spikes, each about an eighth of an inch long and a sixteenth in diameter, with a Velcro fastener instead of shoelaces. Adidas had a shoe called the Quill. It had 42 removable spikes. The legal number of spikes during that time was six per shoe. Several Olympians wore the brush shoe and the quill. Further, the platform divers had hydraulic lifts, which meant that they no longer had to climb in order to dive. So along with the Mexico crisis there were some serious innovations going on, and this was not the end of the chaos surrounding the '68 Olympics.

In February of 1968 the IOC president, Avery Brundage, forgetting Apartheid, readmitted South Africa to the Olympics. Pressure from the Mexicans and the Russians resulted in a special meeting being called in April. Several African nations, Asian nations, and other

157

countries had formed sports associations and they, along with the Russians and the Mexicans, forced Brundage's hand, and the South Africans were kicked out of the games on April 21, 1968.

After the IOC rescinded its invitation to the South Africans, the support of a boycott by blacks was reduced to a meager few. The purpose for the boycott wasn't just based on the fact that South Africa was invited to participate in the Olympics--it was to fight for human rights, and stand against racism and economic depression for all peoples. Harry was more than adamant about having an Olympic boycott because he continued to give speeches and hold conferences, sometimes alone. He met with the athletes in June at USC and in Tahoe in September of '68, but he never went to Mexico where the action was in October '68.

Harry was very visible, and anybody that was visible in the media and made a statement about boycotting became a target of the white racists: he might receive threatening phone calls and hate mail. Tommy Smith, Harry Edwards, Lee Evans, and John had received death threats. Harry had an incident occur at his house. Some white racists took a big black dog, tied a noose around its neck, killed it, then placed it in front of Harry's door -- a warning to Harry that he was possibly next. This happened a month or two before the Olympics. John spoke with Harry who began to talk about how his life was being threatened. He said that he was not going to the Olympics because of the threats, and the killing of the dog was the icing on the cake for him.

I thought about the situation. Shit, all of us have been threatened, and we are going to Mexico where we will be in the open for anyone to shoot at us at any time. So why punk out and give the white racists the privilege of knowing that they put fear in your heart? I had no fear, and I was disappointed with Harry from that point on.

Back to Trinidad

In March of '68, two weeks after the meeting with Dr. Edwards and Dr. King, John was invited to compete again in Trinidad for the Amateur Athletic Union. It was a two-week trip, and another trying time for him. Two tragic events occurred that April. When Dr. King was assassinated, John had been with him no more than ten days prior to his death. The news came to them by radio just before a track meet began. John was devastated! The Trinidadians had a flag-raising ceremony before the race; the British, Australian, German, and other nations' flags flew at half-mast in honor of Dr. King, but not the American. John said that the manager of the team was an old white guy who had distaste for Dr. King, saying, "King wasn't a President, dignitary, or hero for the United States of America. So why should we lower the flag in his honor?" Becoming upset, John went over to the American Flagpole, lowering the flag to half-mast. Leon Coleman, another Olympic sprinter, was with him. While John lowered the flag, Leon broke down into a martial arts stand, and dared anyone to come near it. John replied the manager was upset about John lowering the flag, threatening to write him up and submit it to the AAU committee.

If you touch this flag, I will kick your ass! All of the countries represented here--the Trinidadians, British, Germans, Australians, and other countries--had made known their sentiment for Dr. King, and you mean to tell me that you don't want to allow the American Flag to stand at half mast for an American. As I said, Leon and I are ready to kick your ass about messing with this flag.

The manager knew that Leon and John meant business, and he went along with their demands. Leon (Duma) Coleman commented on this event:

John and I felt compelled to do something about the fact that the manager did not want to lower the flag at half mast. John and I immediately agreed that it had to be lowered. So while John lowered the flag, I broke down into a martial arts stand to make sure that no one messed with John as the flag was lowered. The next day there was an article about the event in Trinidad's newspaper with a photo of me breaking down in that martial arts stand. After everything was said and done, the people from Trinidad and other countries thanked John and I for taking a stand to lower the American flag.

The second tragedy occurred on the track where the sprinters ran. In the USA every major track and field program has one of the following kinds of tracks: clay, asphalt, dirt, or tartan. John had run on all of them. Trinidad had a grass track. The climate in Trinidad is hot and humid, and sometimes it gets so hot that the ground bursts open and make holes in the ground. The sprinters use spikes to dig into the ground to propel them faster; this could pose a problem if the ground isn't stable. While running in a race, John got his cleat entangled in a hole in the grass; he used great force to pull his leg out, and by doing so pulled his right hamstring. He said that it was a painful tear that required immediate treatment. Ice, heat, ultrasound, and massage were used as treatments along with light jogs. He healed quickly due to his youth. The injury took place at the end of the first week. But he remained in Trinidad for the entire two weeks; when he returned to New York, he continued to use the treatments while he jogged each day.

Boycott and Controversy Continue

There was division amongst the athletes because many of them had trained years to have a chance to compete in the Olympics, and they were not willing to give up that opportunity. They decided to run in the Olympics and continued to meet to determine what they would do to make a statement. John was simply waiting to see what the majority would do.

I interviewed Dr. Kirk Clayton, a sprinter from Speed City, and he said that he could have run in the '68 Olympics, but he flat out refused to run for America. He saw the hypocrisy that went along with the false dreams and he returned to university to earn his college education. He spoke to many of the athletes, telling them that if they were going to run for America they must do something by wearing an emblem or making a gesture on the victory stand to demonstrate their disfavor with racism in America. Dr. Clayton told me that he had exposed Tommy Smith and John Carlos to what he would do if he were to participate in the Olympics. As Dr. Clayton said, "I took Tommy and John into my room and I showed them a picture of a fist on my wall that was painted by a friend of mine named Henry Smothers. I told him that if I was to go to the Olympics and I made it to the victory stand, I would make a gesture with a fist. The cargo handlers at the airport lost the picture of the fist that I had on the wall. I was very disappointed about the loss. Tommy and John may not remember the incident, but it did happen!"

The 80-year-old millionaire Avery Brundage was again using his influence to keep amateur status and professional status separated so that the various committees could collect the money that the athletes rightfully deserved. The athletes were competing for America around the world, earning lunch money. Some of them had families, and they could not earn money using their athletic skills under the rules of amateur status. As John recalled,

> I walked into several stadiums around the world, and sometimes there would be 50 to 80 thousand people in there chanting my name; I wasn't collecting a half a cent off any ticket sales, knowing that a great percentage that had attended the stadium came to see me run. So I had to hustle to take care of my family while the Olympic Committee's members became wealthy.

Due to Mexico City's altitude of 7,350 feet, the US Olympic committee decided to conduct the preliminaries for track and field in June in Los Angeles. John had by then healed from his nasty hamstring tear. Around this time twenty-six black male athletes met at USC to discuss the boycott. Not reaching a unanimous decision, the majority decided to participate in the prelims to qualify for the Olympics. John ran his first comeback race June 1, 1968, in San Diego, California.

The athletes who qualified for the Olympics were invited to train in South Lake Tahoe where the altitude is very similar to Mexico's. The final trials were held at Echo Summit, in September of 1968. A meeting was held at this time and the black athletes decided that each person could make a statement by wearing or doing something symbolic on the victory stand. There was not a consensus on that issue, so everyone kind of backed off and concentrated on qualifying for the official trials. Harry Edwards attended both meetings, but many became disinterested in what he had to say about continuing the Olympic boycott. So basically there was a falling away from him by the majority of athletes.

Tahoe

Tahoe is a very beautiful place to work out in the early morning. You can hear the birds singing while the sun changes the light from a dark opaque to brilliant colors bursting with illumination. The Olympic Committee built a tartan track in the middle of a pine forest. While running around the track the athletes would disappear from view.

There were several great athletes who trained at Echo Summit Camp for the Olympic trials in Tahoe: Lee Evans, Jimmy Hines, Ron Coleman, Bob Beamon, Ralph Boston, Willie Davenport, Mel Pender, Kirk Clayton, Ronnie Ray Smith, Erv Hall, Ron Freeman, Vince Matthews, Larry James, and Charlie Green. John had a work ethic that was very demanding, and he ran in any type of weather. He ran in rain, snow, and heat, low or high elevation. It was rather amazing that the black athletes that ran the sprints and hurdles were not affected by running in a high-altitude climate. On the other hand, the distance runners were affected by it tremendously.

John represented the Puma Shoe Company. He promoted their products at every track and field event by wearing their shoes, hats, warm-ups, and anything that they made. As I mentioned earlier, Puma was introducing their new shoe--the Brush Shoe, designed specifically for the tartan track. When John ran the 200-meter race to qualify for the Olympics, all of the top sprinters were in attendance, including Tommy Smith. John was experimenting with the Brush Shoe, and he decided to run the qualifying race in them. On the day of the race he was very relaxed, joking around, putting what he calls the hustle on everyone by talking about how bad he was going to defeat them. This was the typical John Carlos before any race.

When the officials called the runners to the track John had already run the race in his head. The thin air was calm and the sun beamed down on the trees giving off the fresh scent of pine. Only the first four runners to cross the finish line would be able to participate in the Olympics. The voice of the official set them on their marks and the gun shot was a go. John sucked up the cool pine air to come off the blocks before anyone could move. By the time he raised up to a vertical position, using his peripheral vision he saw no one on either side of him. He couldn't hear the grunts and groans of his competitors behind him because he was too far ahead of the pack. Everything was a blur except the finish line. The will to defeat the best in the world, the fresh air, and the chance to give a gesture of protest on the victory stand in the Olympics were real motivations to win big. John crossed the finish line, setting a New World record. He ran a 19.7 in the 200-meter race. When the officials learned that John had worn Brush Shoes to run the race, the International Amateur Athletic Federation made a ruling on the case: Brush Shoes were illegal; thus his world's record was disqualified. Nonetheless, he was qualified to participate in the Olympics.

Prior to the Olympic preliminaries, John had been terrorizing track and field, losing only once in 18 straight races. He also had won six straight Most Valuable Performer Awards. Holding the title "Fastest Man in the World," he had defeated the best in the world in the 100 and the 200-yard dash. He could have run in the 100,

WHY? The Biography of John Carlos

200, 4x100 relay and/or the 400 meters. He was the top qualifier, and he could have won a gold medal in each of the events.

The Olympians had 30 days to prepare themselves for the games. There were lots of activities in that time. The first day of that period began with the athletes being fitted for their Olympic attire; they were flown to Denver, Colorado where a meeting was held with all of the black athletes. According to Willie Davenport, a gold medal winner in the high hurdles, that particular meeting was the most memorable and important because there was unity there. Having been alerted about the boycott activities, the FBI and CIA had created files on the participants. After the meeting they approached John and several other Olympians.

> The agents came out to our practices, and they tried to buy our allegiance by promising us that if we did not protest, we could get anything that we wanted. They reminded us that the NFL, Hollywood, big businesses, and other areas of the financial world would be available to us if we kept our mouths shut. They mentioned that people like Jim Brown, Sydney Poitier, and Sammy Davis Jr. would soon need to be replaced with some new blood. They created a scene that would entice the weak materialistic individual who can't see that truth, justice, and equality is greater than riches! All they had to do was keep their mouths shut, and money would come their way. Further, agents mentioned that we should seriously concentrate on de-

feating the Cubans and the Russians. It seemed that they had a vested interest in us doing so. My response was that I would rather be poor than to be bought like a slave to speak when the master says to speak for their riches. I survive because God has given me that right, and he provides everything for me. I refused their offer!

They remained in Denver for a couple of days, and from there they flew to Mexico City.

While on the plane, John said, he reflected on what was happening in America and the world. America was going through one of the greatest protest times in its history: 1968 was the year of the protest! Dr. King had been shot and killed in April because he protested against the injustices in America. Bobby Kennedy had been slain at the Ambassador Hotel in Los Angeles after giving a speech about his platform as a presidential candidate. The universities across the nation were protesting the war in Vietnam. Richard Nixon was elected president to do away with Lyndon B. Johnson's Great Society because the conservative right wing Republicans were complaining that LBJ was giving blacks and other minorities too much money through social programs. The National Guard killed several students at Kent State University. The first black Student Union was created on San Jose State University's campus which, by the way, was the first UC campus, founded in California in 1857. Blacks were complaining that the curriculum in the schools, colleges, and universities did not discuss contributions by blacks, browns, Indians and Asians. From that spark, black Student Unions sprang up across the nation and the concept of Ethnic Studies was introduced to the nation.

Dr. Maulana Karenga, the creator of the African American and Pan African Holiday, Kwanzza, played a vanguard role in developing the black Power Movement, Black Studies, Afrocentricity, and the Black Student Union Movement. Womens' organizations were on the rise. They were demanding the same equal rights as white males. The Black Panther Party was creating terror in the white establishment with its leaders H. Rap Brown and Eldridge Cleaver, the author of *Soul on Ice*. The Panthers demanded reparations or payment from the U.S. government for the injustices that slavery placed upon blacks in America. The Muslims, led by Elijah Mohammed, had a strong presence as the Nation of Islam labored to become independent from the white establishment. They, like the Panthers, helped to reform ex-cons, dope dealers, pimps, gang-bangers, prostitutes, and others in society. They also developed schools, breakfast programs, newspapers, job training programs, jobs, and hope. The racist media portrayed these organizations as hate groups never doing anything well. But as one can see, they reformed individuals that state institutions, prisons and others could not reform. Freedom, justice, and equality were being demanded by the masses across the nation. The black athletes had seen and heard all of the things that I mentioned above, and the bottom line was that they knew that they were not going to boycott the Olympics, and the question was: What are you going to do to make a statement?

Mexico City

The United States Olympic Team arrived in Mexico City's airport as a team. They were there at last! And for 90% of them, it was total excitement. John had visited Mexico City in 1967, when, he said, poverty was at an all-time high.

When I got off the plane on my first visit I could see the poverty right outside of the airport. So I knew about the conditions of the people in terms of Mexico having slums and ghettos. There were no middle-class people. The economic situation was that the rich had all of the money while the majority of the people lived in poverty. Mothers breast-fed their babies on the streets while begging for money for them. Children ran around begging for money, and when one would ask and you reached in your pocket to give him or her money, at least 10 to 20 more would come from nowhere with their hands out. Many people were sleeping on the hard sidewalk because they had nowhere else to go. Pro-stitution, drugs, and alcohol were common-place. There were some of the most beautiful girls you've ever seen that would come and ask you to have sex with them for a few dollars. The situation was quite disturbing.

John wondered if the Mexican government, the USA, and the Olympic Committee would bring about a change with all of the money that was pumped into Mexico. To his surprise, when they got off the airplane in Mexico City, the Mexicans had built a fence around the airport area. The Mexicans placed large beautifully colored Olympic banners, flags, and advertisements all over the place. While many admired the beauty, John walked over to the fence and looked to see if the Mexicans had cleaned up the slum area.

> They hadn't done a damn thing. The poverty situation was still there, and the grass root people received nothing from all of the money that came into the country. It is a damn shame that the International Committee and the Mexicans had one interest, and that was to earn money for those who already had it.

When they boarded the large buses waiting to carry them to the Olympic Village, John observed how excited every one was. From his observations he came to the conclusion that each one of them had every right to fulfill their dreams of being a part of the Olympic Games. They had prepared all of their lives to get there, and a boycott should not interfere with their dreams of becoming Olympic Champions.

John said that the Olympic Village had almost a college campus atmosphere. The festivities and celebration were tops. Every moment was like a new experience. Upon their arrival, they could see and hear a large band playing Mexican music. People dressed in festive colors-beautiful red, green and white costumes representing the Mexican flag--danced to the folklore rhythms of Mexican music. And there were teams from other countries dressed in their festive attire. It was quite a spectacle to see all of the beautiful colors at the same time. During the time that all of the festivities were going on other teams arrived too. So the Mexicans welcomed and celebrated countries for several days. In all there were 107 teams represented.

While observing the activities, everyone gathered their things. They noticed that there were Mexican soldiers walking around the place with machine guns. This did not deter anyone and they got off the bus and walked to their assigned buildings. They entered a tall brown four-story building where the athletes were assigned to rooms. John's roommate was Bob Beamon, a long jumper from Harlem. He and John had met in New York when they were kids. They got themselves settled in very quickly because they were interested in checking out the variety of women Olympians. There were women from Africa, India, Europe, Asia, and elsewhere. They walked around in their ethnic colors in top shape and form. It seemed that each one of them walked proudly, saying I am the number one person from my country, and I am proud of that. John said that the women were exception-ally beautiful. Respect and admiration permeated the place as each team strutted their stuff. Everyone on the US team knew that the Americans were the number-one team in the world.

When the African nations arrived something magical happened.

The African nations knew about the black Americans' plight regarding the Olympic boy-cott. From that understanding they developed a great respect for what we had done. But most importantly they were happy that we decided to participate. They esteemed us highly, and right away there came into being a confirm- ation that the Africans would win all of the long distance races and the Americans would win the short distance races. Further, when the Cubans came and blacks from other countries arrived, there was an instant bond. It was not about governments and things; it was about human beings meeting and coming together as friends. It was about black athletes coming together as friends.

All of the black athletes from every different country bonded together. The black athletes were there to let every one know that they did not boycott the games, but they were there to set a precedent that no white athletes were going to win anything. It was like an unspoken word among the blacks; it was in the air. From that point, it was no longer an American Olympics; it became a black Olympics. It wasn't about a black American, Cuban, or African. It was about being black! It was a black thing! It was universal! As blacks, we were presenting ourselves to the world as one. That is what the unity was all about.

After everyone got settled, a flag-raising ceremony took place for each country that participated in the Olympics. So the Americans met outside the dorms, and they walked over together to the flag pole area where the American flag would be raised. The Australians,

Germans, and the Japanese had their flag ceremony along with the USA. A large Mexican
band played each country's national anthem.
Again brilliant colors, and pomp and circumstance prevailed, and many individuals stood
tall while their anthems were being played.
The festivity did not last very long because
everyone had to be indoctrinated into the
entire Olympic system. So after the ceremonies,
it was time to get educated as to what was
going on.

Every athlete, coach, referee, judge, lane manager,
time keeper, set-up crew member, track measurer, trainer,
reporter, TV crew, photographer, and many others had
to learn their parts in this world event very quickly. It
was a time to take mental notes right from the start
because one mistake could cost someone everything. In
other words, if participants did not know what time their
race began and they missed it, they would not get a
second chance.

Further, you had to take into account how the
facilities were run, where the towels were, stores,
cafeteria, training times, bed checks, free time, clean up
times for rooms, check in and check out times in the
Olympic Village, schedules to run their events, and many
other things.

Once John found out all of the essential things that
he needed to know he and some other friends hit the
town to find out where the clubs were. But before they
left the Village, they found out that they had a curfew to
adhere to. So John approached the assistant Olympic
track coach Stan Wright:

Coach, I have no disrespect towards you or coach Jordan, the head coach, but I am not going to live in the Olympic Village for the duration of the Olympics because my wife is coming to town. When she arrives, we will share a room together somewhere else. As far as the curfew is concerned, all of us are grown men, and I come and go as I please. Coach, you know that I never allow anything to interfere with my training. I am always in top form.

Coach Wright and Coach Jordan understood the situation, and they were OK with John's decisions. John remained in the village for three days, and his wife had not arrived. On the third day, he ran into an old friend of his named Mel Zahn. Mel was a portly, Jewish self-made millionaire that John met when he was a kid running for the New York Pioneer Club. John said that Mel was a very likable guy, and whatever Mel had he shared it with others. Mel had purchased a large private villa near the Olympic Village, and he invited John and his wife to live there during the games. Mel also invited Bob and his wife too. John said that Bob wasn't there with his wife; he was there with a woman who posed as his wife. He also went around telling everyone that the woman was his wife. This would pose a problem later.

The villa was extremely large with at least 15 rooms, housed behind a large brick wall where one had to go through a large gate to enter. There were servants, cooks, and gardeners on the premises to take care of everything. Mel felt compelled to share this with his friends. John said that the hospitality was like nothing that he had experienced, and he will always love and respect Mel for his kindness.

John had moved from the Olympic Village to a mansion with servants. He said that he was kicking back thinking about the fact that his parents had never seen him run a race. Many of the other athletes had their parents there, and he thought about how nice it would be to have his parents in that villa with him enjoying the spice of life. Many people had said that John Carlos wasn't going to amount to anything, and here he was participating in an event that was being televised everywhere on the earth. There are people in the world that would do most anything to have the opportunity to participate in the Olympic Games. But John Carlos, the son of Earl and Vioris Carlos was a participant, and it would have been so nice to have them to experience the moment with him. John said that he never revealed the thought about having his parents there with him until now, 30 years later.

John talked about the Mexican student protest:

I will never forget the mass murder per-petrated by the Mexican Government on the students who protested. I was exposed to the situation a day before I arrived in Mexico. I watched the protest from TV too. There were thousands of students protesting with signs, making gestures, and shouting their differences in Spanish. Strong opposition against the government and the Olympics was voiced, and they hoped to use the world stage of the Olympics to voice their plight on a global network. The Mexican Army would see it differently. This was the first time that a third world country had ever hosted an Olympic Games. There was a lot of money to be earned too, and the Mexican government did not want to lose their profits. They did not want to fail under any circumstances, even at the expense of killing their own people.

As the Olympics neared, the student protest became national with TV cameras and reporters on the frontlines recording the protests. The Mexican students never envisioned that the government's will was to host the Olympics at any cost. From their military camp just outside Mexico City the Mexican army drove into downtown by the truckload, bringing machine guns and other kinds of weapons, because making sure that the Olympic Games took place without incident was a matter of national pride, national security, and national honor. They lined up in front of the students, and conversations took place. The army officials must have given them an ultimatum to leave or be shot, for when the students did not move, the soldiers were ordered to fire into the crowd.

They shot them down like dogs. Bodies lay everywhere and pools of blood were in the streets. Students by the hundreds were running for their lives, while those who weren't so fortunate lay dead or wounded. It was dis-covered later that the soldiers took some of the bodies and threw them in an incinerator to be burned in a factory near by while others found themselves in a watery grave in the Pacific Ocean. Those who remained alive were carried off to jail and/or in the mountains until the games were over. It is possible that they killed many on the way to jail. There were at least around 1500 to 2000 students shot and/or killed. The Mexican newspaper did not report the incident as a major catastrophe. The government tried to suppress the killing, and I do know that no one was brought to justice for the crime of mass murder. I arrived in Mexico a few days after the mass murder occur-red. As soon as I got situated, I went out and I talked to the people on the streets about the protest. I got very good information as to what took place.

In the Home Box Office (HBO) Documentary *Fists of Freedom*, Bob Paul, the Press Secretary for the Olympic Committee, was interviewed. The Associated Press in New York called Paul to report on the mass genocide in Mexico City. After they reported the event, they asked him if the Olympians and officials were going to go to Mexico as scheduled. Press Secretary Paul said, "We will be on that plane to arrive in Mexico at 8:00 tomorrow." He made no comment about the deaths of the students. They meant nothing to him! To him, the death of those students was like killing a hog, a cow, and Niggers. He expressed no feelings, no sympathy, let the games begin. Had those been white students from the United States, the Games would have been postponed until further notice.

The American dollar was like gold in Mexico. A person could buy many things due to the great difference in the exchange rate. The Mexican merchants and street vendors knew this, and they capitalized on it. They sold everything from the traditional sombrero, serapes, pyramids, gold, silver, and piñatas, to every kind of Olympic emblem. They had merchants and vendors on every corner asking people to come into their stores to buy things. Most of them were selling the same products. John and his friends bought several items, and he said that he wished he could have purchased something from all of the merchants. The people on the streets who begged from them were given money on demand, and it was hard for John and friends who were concerned about their needs. Overall, the tours and shopping activities were good for him because it was a positive way to get away from thinking about the tremendous pressure that he and others with him were under.

Training

During all of this activity, the Olympians were training to fine-tune themselves before the 30 days terminated, and the Olympic competition began. John stated that he had made a deal with his coach Stan Wright in Tahoe during the Olympic Trials. The deal was that if John could put together a B Team to defeat the A Team in the 4x400 meter relay 2 out of 3 times, he would allow him to run the relay for the Olympic team. John put a B team together with Tommy Smith and they defeated the A team 2 out of 3 times. The coach was amazed at what the B team had done. The deal was real, and it was time for Coach Wright to pay up. John confronted the coach about the deal because during the Olympic training time he was not selected to run.

I wasn't given a chance to compete in the 100, 4x100 relay, and/or the 400-meters. I realized that I had not run in those events during the regular track season, but I was permitted to run in them during the preliminaries. I defeated everyone. I felt that since I was allowed to compete in the events during the preliminaries, I should have a chance to compete in them during the Olympics. Coach Wright had his own man Jimmy Hines from Texas Southern University to run the 100-yard dash. Hilmer Lodge was the clerk in charge of the entry committee; he made sure that the top qualifiers in each Olympic category were placed correctly in each event. I believe that he and Stan made a discussion as to who was going to run in the 100 and the other events. In doing so, they decided that John Carlos was not going to run in them even though he had the fastest times in all of the events. I strongly believe that this is what kept me from competing in those events. I had dominated the 200-yard dash, and the decision was to allow me to compete in that event alone.

Coach Wright explained to John that he did not have the authority to allow him to compete in the 4x400 meter relay. Coach Wright was a father figure to John, and it hurt him to have to tell John that he could not keep his word about the deal. And John was very disappointed, but he forgave the coach and continued to train.

About this time, Avery Brundage, the International Olympic Committee President, began to wield his authority by sending messages to John saying that he better not attempt any kind of protest, trouble, or demonstration. John did not pay the message or messengers any mind because he knew that he was going to do something to let the world know about the hypocrisy, poverty, and the second-class treatment that blacks had to endure in America.

The Olympic Committee and the US Government pumped more bullshit messages at the black athletes than a septic tank could hold. The US Military sent telegrams too because there were blacks that were in the military while they ran for the Olympics. Mel Pender, a sprinter, a participant in the 1964 Olympics in Japan, and a military man, had been involved with the protest meetings. The US Government scrutinized him. He

John Carlos with CD Jackson

received a threatening telegram from the government saying that he better not participate in any kind of protest during the games. It also stated that if he did, they would send him to the front line of the Vietnam War. John read the telegram, stating that it was real disturbing and threatening. Neither Mel nor John ever thought that the military would put a man in such a life-threatening position. After John summed up his thoughts about the telegram, he told Mel that the government was going to send him to the front line anyway. "So do what you feel is right for you," John told him. In time, John's word became true because after the Olympic Games Mel was sent to Vietnam. Willie Davenport, the Olympic high hurdler, was a military man, and John believed that he was in the military during the time of the Olympics. If so, he no doubt received the same telegram that Mel had. The black athletes received threats on every end. They had to be seriously motivated and disciplined to continue to focus on their athletic goals.

John's roommate Bob Beamon, an Olympic long jumper, fell outside of the discipline category due to some personal problems. John said that Bob barely made the Olympic team by placing third as an Olympic qualifier. Concerned about Bob's problem, he had offered to train him at Echo Summit in Lake Tahoe. John explained to Bob that he wasn't jumping far because his speed and form were weak. He explained that an airplane had to build up tremendous speed in order to leap and break away from gravity in order to fly. The long jump required the same concept. He also reminded Bob about the times that they used to run along side one another as kids in Harlem. Also Bob was a sprinter before he was a long jumper, running at speeds below 9.5

seconds in the hundred. Bob's memory of what John said to him gave him confidence. He was elated over the fact that John had reminded him of his abilities, and he eagerly accepted an offer from John to train him in the long jump.

In Mexico City John continued his work with Bob Beamon, teaching him how to control his speed, form, steps, and how to discipline his mind to allow the jump to come naturally. Leon Coleman, an Olympic sprinter, also worked out with Bob and John. First John taught them to listen to the sound of the gun. They would have a timer with a gun to set them off within four tenths of a second, and then bang you take off. They did it at two tenths of a second. If they jumped the gun, they would do 15 to 20 push-ups on the spot as a discipline. They built up their upper body strength by doing this. The push-ups also extracted some of their energy; thus they had to concentrate more on technique. That is why it was imperative to train for a variety of times. He also taught them to listen for the gun while running because some of their lives had been threatened.

In about three weeks, Bob worked himself into excellent shape. He got to the point that he could run about 9.3 sec. in the hundred-yard dash. From that point, John worked on calculating his steps to a new rhythm. John worked on all aspects of Bob Beamon's game, and the results would prove to be a milestone for him. Leon's speed had improved too. After the gruesome workouts each day, every one of them went out and had some fun.

Mexico, population-wise, is the largest city in the world, and there were always people around and something to do. He also took advantage of the rich culture and history in Mexico. He and others went out into the countryside to see the beautiful landscape, the awesome pyramid of the sun and moon, old churches, and the Presidential Palace. There was some construction going on in the city while he toured, and he noticed that the workers were tearing down high-rise buildings. To his surprise they didn't have power tools like the ones he was accustomed to seeing in New York. The workers tore the building down with hammers and chisels. This kind of blew John's mind, and he said, "Wow, these people are going to be working for a long time." But the one thing that they had was the manpower, and people had a job. The Mexicans did not allow new technology to interfere with their idea of labor nor their concept of time.

Trying to obtain information about a possible protest, the world press was interviewing many of the Olympians. John said that they were roaming around like bears trying to find honey in the woods. The press was represented in all areas of the Olympic Village. John completed interviews with many of them. No one chaired the meetings. Ralph Boston, a long jumper, was a senior Olympian and he took some leadership in the meetings which were open to the press, and to all black athletes from around the world. The urgency to have the meetings was to clear the air so that there would not be any animosity between those who chose to boycott and those who did not choose to boycott. The discussions went well and the friction aired out. But they could not come to a consensus as to what they would do as a group because when a suggestion was made it was shot down. For example, someone said that they should wear black shoes. Several of the athletes were being paid to wear shoes; so that idea was thrown out. So in the last meeting it was decided that "everyone would do his or her own thing."

John carried a boom box around everywhere he went. While he was walking around in the village a young Mexican kid jumped over the hedges because he was late to work. Inadvertently he bumped into John's arm, knocking the boom box out of his hand. The boom box broke. John became a little disturbed about the situation, and he grabbed the kid. Looking at him he could see that he had had no intentions of jumping into him so he allowed the kid to go. There were several people around that saw what went on. Some people commented on how well he handled the situation. But the next day the newspaper stated that John Carlos was walking around with his music so loud that the people wanted to destroy his box. They said that the kid who destroyed his box was assisting the ones that wanted to get rid of the alleged noise. They indicated that he wanted to beat the kid down and make him pay for the box. The story was totally untrue; it was simply a character assassination.

With the utmost respect and favor, John talked about the black female Olympians. He said that they never received proper recognition as world-class athletes, and as great contributors to the proposed 1968 boycott. He mentioned Madeline Manning, the 800-meter gold medal winner. He said that she was the first and the last women's 800-meter winner in the U.S. before and after the 1968 Olympics 32 years later, Ms. Manning complimented John at a ceremony celebrating former Olympics during the 2000 Olympic trials in Sacramento, stating that John was the first to bring entertainment to track and field. He mentioned Wyomia Tyus, the 1964 gold medal winner in the 100-meter in Tokyo. She also returned to participate in the 1968 Olympics. There was no serious recognition for this great feat. Then he gave me a list of other African American females who participated in the 1968 Olympics: Margaret Johnson Bailes, Estelle Baskervill, Iris Davis, Barbara Farrell, Mamie Rallins, Jarvis Scott, Ester Stroy, Martha Rae Watson, and Willye White. John said that these black women showed a tremendous amount of strength, fortitude, intelligence, and great athletic ability. They had great character, personality, sportsmanship, and overall class, but they did not receive the credit and recognition for being the outstanding individuals that they were.

John said that the media and press looked at the women as if they were flies on an elephant's ass, not worth mentioning. He said that the media, the Olympic Committee, the press, Harry Edwards and any one else that wrote about the 1968 Olympics and prior to it was sexist. They could not see the importance of recognizing the greatness in these women in the world of sports. He said that he was in awe of them, and could not understand how they could have been ignored. He has always supported the women, and he has the highest respect and admiration for all of the sisters that were Olympians.

Opening Day

The Opening Day ceremony began on Sunday, October 12, 1968. The Mexican newspaper was headlined "Grandioso." A hundred teams marched into the Olympic stadium; each dressed in their country's colors, led by a respected Olympian holding their flag. The costumes and flags showed magnificent colors. The band played songs in the universal language called music. The photographers took thousands of photos with their expensive cameras. The TV cameras scanned across the stadium to record each team as they entered, and 80,000 people in the stadium and people around the world cheered them on.

It wasn't a question about whether or not I wanted to wear the Olympic uniform: a red blazer, blue shirt, and white pants in the opening ceremony. I did not come there for a parade, so I wasn't going to get into one. My whole purpose for being there was to make a statement. Pieces of the puzzle were coming together in my mind. What I mean by the pieces of the puzzle is that I was checking out what Avery Brundage was doing, the U.S. Olympic Officials, the attitudes of the different athletes, the peoples who were poor and starving, the Mexican students that were assassinated, the number of people who paid to get into the stadium, the lack of money the athletes were given, the gold, silver, and bronze medals were not made of their material names. They were fake!

I began to reflect on my childhood vision at age seven when God showed me a stadium where people cheered for me while I stood on a platform, and suddenly without a cause known to me, they booed me. All of these things were coming together in my mind, and I knew that I was there to make a statement. So I went to Tommy Smith and I told him that I was not going to the opening ceremony, and I also explained why. He responded to what I said by saying, "If you aren't going to go, I'm not going either." I said cool! I also ran into Leon Coleman, Ron Freeman, and some more Olympians, and they were all excited, saying, "Hey Los, come on and get dressed. Aren't you going?" I said, "Naw, man, I think I'm going to pass." There was a TV room in the village; Tommy and I watched the opening ceremony with some other Olympians that had to compete the same day. The same enthusiasm that I saw expressed in the black athletes was demonstrated on the TV. In my mind I can see Ron Freeman walking into the stadium with a big smile waving to all his friends back home when he knew that the TV cameras were on him. Then there was Randy Mattson, a big strong robust man walking, expressing joy and jubilation. Randy was a world record holder in the shot put. Wyomia Tyus, a sprinter and 4x4 hundred-meter gold medal winner was walking in proudly for a second Olympics. I gathered strength from each participant's enthusiasm, and God revealed to me that they deserved to have their dreams come true. I also felt that I would have the chance to fulfill my dream, and that was to get on that victory stand and make that statement. I was happy for them.

John said that he asked himself a question after the ceremony. The question was had he missed anything. That was a great spectacle he observed, and he could have been a part of it. But had he gone he would never have gotten the opportunity to watch all of his friends enjoy themselves so much, and he wouldn't have gathered strength had he not observed their joy.

The first day began with track and field. The Africans dominated the long distance run. They won the 1,500-meter, 5,000-meter, 10,000-meter, and the Marathon. Jim Ryan, an American, was the world record holder for the 1500- meter, which turned out to be one of the most spectacular races in the Olympics. He was favored to win, but the Africans would see things differently. The Africans developed a plan to defeat Jim by putting the rabbit concept on him. The rabbit concept was to have a guy who is least likely to win run as fast as he could to lead the pack, while the guy who is favored to win conserves his energy by following the guy in front (the rabbit) until a certain point in the race, then he uses his conserved energy to sprint out from behind to replace the rabbit about 400 meters, into the race. Ben Jiipcho was the rabbit for the Kenyans, and Kipchoge Keino followed. They left everyone behind. Jim Ryan ran almost last in the race. When the rabbit Ben ran past 400 meters, the damage was done in terms of providing Kip with the right pace in order to defeat Jim. When Kip Keino ran across the finish line, Jim Ryan was 25 yards behind. John had respect for Jim as a man and athlete, but when all of the black athletes from around the world sat together that day to watch the race he rooted for Kip Keino. They had made a pact that the Africans would win the long distance races and the Americans would win the short distance. So there was not one black in the group that was not pulling for the Africans to win. Kip Keino's illustrious 1500-meter race put the icing on the cake. Ultimately the Olympics, for the blacks, became a black Olympics.

All of the black athletes from around the world sat together in the Olympic stadium: The Jamaicans, Ghanaians, Ugandans, Kenyans, Nigerians, Americans, Puerto Ricans, Cubans, and people from the Bahamas. They were playing the steel drums, congas, and other instruments, singing and laughing and talking, enjoying themselves to the max. The smell of food permeated the area as they passed food to one another. The atmosphere was radiant, and filled with joy. The energy was so high that it was explosive. Many people looked on, never truly understanding what was going on. There was unity among blacks from around the world!

On Monday, October 13, 1968, John was seated in the stands around nine o'clock as he watched the preliminary heat for the 100-meter. The top three contenders were James Hines, Lennox Miller of Jamaica, and Charlie Green. The competitors who ran in the 100, 200,

400, sprint relay, and the mile relay had to compete in a preliminary heat, round 2, semi-final, and the final race for the medals. John had defeated all of the top competitors in the 100-meter in the Olympic Trials, but he had established himself as the best in the 200-meter. Not allowed to run the 100-meter due to politics, he had to sit and watch with disappointment. Nonetheless he under-stood the situation and never held a grudge against anyone.

John had to run the 200 preliminary heat that same day, which he won effortlessly. After the race, he got involved with all of the activities that took place in and around the village. He mingled with Kip Keino, 1500-meter gold medallist, and Abebe Bikila, winner of the gold medal Marathon in the 1960 and '64 Olympics, both from Ethiopia. John, being very interested in the history of Ethiopia, had many discussions with Kip and Abebe about Ethiopia's history. John had a particular interest in Haile Salassie, the king who traced his lineage to Jesus Christ and King Solomon.

John became acquainted with Abebe because he wore Puma Shoes. He was very fond of Abebe because he was a warm, kind man who was very humble. He always had something positive to say, and he was open and honest, not fearing to speak the truth. John also developed a relationship with the Mexican workers in the village. He would go in and talk to them about their life, and he would share stories with them. Further, he recorded interviews with the world press every day. They were subject to come around at any time in and out of the village.

As I mentioned before, John and Bob Beamon had moved into a villa with Mel Zane. On the day of the 100-

meter preliminary heat, Bob's wife Bertha arrived in Mexico. She was searching for Bob and ran into John somewhere around the village. John explained:

> Somehow Bob's wife Bertha got some good information that Bob had been seen with another woman, and the woman wasn't her. She told me in certain terms that she had something with her, and someone was going to get hurt. She asked me if I had seen him, and I said no. I hadn't seen Bob that day, but I had an idea where he was. I didn't give her any information because of what she told me. I had to think about the idea that she might hurt Bob, maybe even herself, and myself. I also wondered if the incident would affect Bob's performance, because I trained him. So immediately I found Bob and I told him that Bertha was in town. After that, I told him what she said. He was very concerned, and he thanked me for the information. I did what I had to do, and left it at that!

The following day John competed in round 2 in the 200-meter, easily winning again. He felt good about the race, but needed to talk to Tommy about something of great importance. The response he received would determine how he should run the final race.

Semi-Final Race, and A Plan

On the day of the semi-final race, John won with decisively. Prior to the race, John had had a conversation with Tommy Smith. John described the conversation:

"Hey, Tommy, I want to talk to you about something."

"OK, Los."

'Tommy, this is the deal as far as what it is that I want to do on the victory stand. I want to make a statement that means blackness. I mean that everything that we do or wear will be a symbol that says something about the history and the struggle of the black man and black woman. Do you understand where I'm coming from?"

Tommy responded, "OK, Los, I understand, and I am with you." John talked a bit about the struggle in terms of what he was thinking at the time. He put it in this context:

> I wanted to use the protest to raise consciousness about the Olympic Games. I wanted to create a protest to tell the world that the black man and woman dominate the Olympic Games, and this particular Olympics is a black Olympics for blacks all over the world. This protest is a protest to mourn the deaths of all of the black women, men, boys, and girls that died fighting against the European kidnappers on the shores of Africa. Then to those who died in the Middle Passage along the way. Then to those who were beaten unmercifully by the

slave masters, being separated from family, religion, and language.

Since 1952 reparations amount now to 3.5 billion dollars and more than 44 million acres of land have been paid to Japanese Americans, Jewish Claims on Austria, Indians, Eskimos, Japanese Canadians, Ottawas of Michigan, Chippewas, Seminoles of Florida, Sioux, Klamaths of Oregon, Alaska Natives, and German Jews. Black people have lost over 50 to one hundred million people in a span of 400 years of slavery just like the Native American Indians. Black Americans never got anything for the mistreatment of slavery by America. Somebody had to say something about the mistreatment of black people around the world. Many of the black ministers, politicians, educators, and businessmen weren't doing anything other than conforming to the status quo. They weren't talking about giving up their lives and taking a few so that their children could have it better. The black Panthers did what they could do, but they were shut down real quick. Martin and Malcolm did a great job, but they did not have a world stage until they were long dead. The Olympics gave us a world stage, and we had the opportunity to say something to it while we were being presented a medal on a victory platform. This was exciting to me. So my whole purpose was to use that world stage to represent blackness.

Tommy mentioned to John in the conversation that he had some black gloves that his wife Denise had bought him. John told him to bring them to the final race. John had purchased some black love beads, and he planned to use them as a symbol. The conversation ended, and they went their separate ways.

There was a reason why John asked Tommy to do something with him on the victory platform. The first reason was that Tommy and John had been favored to win a medal. The second reason was that if anything went down during the protest John could protect Tommy's back and Tommy, looking out for him in case anything violent or negative happened, could protect him in turn. So you could say that it was for survival reasons that John asked Tommy to assist him. The gold medal became secondary to the protest statement once Tommy agreed to assist John with his plan.

The 200-Meter Final

The morning of the final race was Wednesday, October 16, 1968. John found a second track somewhere behind the Olympic Stadium. He would hang out sometimes because his free-spirited coach Bud Winters would hang out there too. There were many things going through John's mind and he confided some things to Bud before the final race. He talked about what he was there to do as a man and as an Olympian. He started by asking Bud what he thought about the race. Bud turned around and asked John the same question.

The race don't mean shit to me. I talked to Tommy about making a statement after the race, and he agreed. When he agreed to assist me, the race became secondary. I knew how much the gold medal meant to Tommy, and I wanted to see his dream come true. I felt that a silver medal would be fine with me as long as I get a chance to make a statement. If the medal meant everything to Tommy, he can have the medal. I need him to watch my back and I watch his while we make a statement on the victory stand.

Yes, John, the gold medal means the world to Tommy, and he would be elated if he won it.

Bud knew John well. He knew about his emotions, and what really turned him on when it came to track and field. He knew that he was having fun just being there,

197

and he did not have to win a medal to prove anything to anybody as to who John Carlos is.

John won all of his races that led up to the finals with ease. He said that he was pleased to see the following men from other countries win and get a chance to go to the final 200-meter race: Mike Fray from Jamaica, Roger Bambuck from France, and Edwin Robinson from Trinidad. Larry Questhead, a white kid from Stanford, made it to the finals too. John said that Larry did not have the athletic ability that many of the other athletes had, but he had the determination to stay in the race and qualify. John had much respect for him.

Art Simburg, the Puma Shoe Company representative, had somehow got caught up in customs with the running shoes for the track team. John had run the preliminary heats in his practice shoes. In the final race, he planned to run in his best shoes, but they never arrived. He knew that his friend Ed Caruthers, an Olympic high jumper, wore the same size shoe that he did: a 13. So John found Ed and asked him if he could borrow his shoes to run the final race in. Ed was more than happy to allow him to wear his shoes, which had been stretched from wear and the wet weather. They did not fit snugly, but he at least had something to run in. John explained what took place before the race:

> I had planned to master the race by leading out strong and controlling everyone as I led. I wanted Tommy to have the gold medal, and I knew without a doubt that I would take the silver medal. I did not hustle anyone before this race because this particular race was for me. I became serious about the race final in

Tahoe when I broke the world's record with a
19.7. I know that I was the best in the world,
not only in the 200-meter, but also in the 100-
meter and the 4x4 relay because I had defeated
the best in the world in all of the categories. It
was not a question as to whether John Carlos
was going to win a medal; it was a question as
to what I decided I wanted to win.

There was no one in the world at that time
that could defeat me. I did not know how I was
going to run the 200-meter race, because at the
time of the trials, I had not talked to Tommy
about assisting me with the protest. But I knew
that the medal meant more to him than anything. So I got on the phone in Tahoe, and I
called Jerry Williams in San Jose to tell him that
I had broken the world's records. I told him
that I was going to do it before I left. Then I
called all of my roadies in New York, and I
told them that I broke the world's record, and
not to bet on me in the final race in Mexico. I
told them that this was something personal
and I did not know how I was going to run the
races until I got to Mexico. I was focused on
one thing, and that was to make a statement.

The 200-meter is a very exciting race. The anticipation of seeing it run was extremely high. There were
50,000 people in the stands by this time; many of the
80,000 who had been in attendance had gone to their
homes because it was late in the evening when they ran.
Many of the Mexicans were attracted to John not only as
a great track man with charm and personality but because

of the name Carlos. Several wondered if he was from the Caribbean Islands, Mexico, or South America. Many cheered for him before the race began. The Olympians were stretching, talking, and doing their usual rituals before the race.

The officials had announced the race and all of the participants got in their respective lanes. Tommy was to the left side of me, and I could see him from where I was. The official starter got us ready by saying, "Runners on your marks, get set," and he shot the gun. Boom! I broke off the line quickly. I led the race for the first 130 meters to allow everyone to know that I had the ability to win the race if I wanted to do so. But I chose not to. I shut down my jets to auto pilot around the 140-meter mark. I looked to my left to see if I could see Tommy coming. I did, but it seemed like he was struggling to make the lead. I looked back, and I yelled, "Come on Tommy, and quit bullshitting if you want to win this race." Tommy put on his jets, and man he moved like a gazelle on the African plains. He supposedly had hurt his leg in the semi final race, but he ran as if nothing had ever been wrong. He caught up to me around the 165 meters. When he did that, I knew that I would finish the race like I had planned to.

But to my right, I see this person running right next to me at the 180-meter mark. It was Peter Norman from Australia. It was impossible for me to put the jets on again after running

180 meters, and in a matter of a few seconds Tommy hit the finish line with his hands held high in the air for the victory. Peter Norman and I ran across the finish line at the same time. I had forgotten about Peter's ability to come on strong at the last 20 meters of the race. I had seen him run that kind of a race during the earlier heats. Had I not been so focused on getting Tommy through the race, I would have watched Peter and beat him decisively. After the race, I immediately went over to Tommy and I hugged and congratulated him for the victory. I knew that I had placed, but I felt that Peter had defeated me. I looked at the clock and it stated that Peter and I hit the tape at 20.0 seconds flat. I said to myself right then that if a white man can run a 20 sec. flat in the 200-meter, he deserves to win the second place medal. We were ushered into a tunnel in the Olympic Stadium. Coach Stan Wright came up to me excitedly and said, "John, we got first and second." I told him that he was wrong, that we got first and third. In just a matter of minutes the officials ruled that Peter had taken second. I was satisfied with the decision.

The excitement in the tunnel was high. Many of the athletes from all over the world were talking in different languages about their victories. Stan Wright, Payton Jordan, and all of the Americans in the tunnel were excited. It is hard to explain the joy: a dream of a lifetime had been met for many, and now it was time to reap the harvest. In other words, it was medal time. The press was there talking to various individuals, taking photos, trying to capture the moment. The officials, coaches, information persons, and others were there to give them instructions as to how the medal ceremonies were to be conducted. John, Tommy, and Peter Norman were in the same area of the tunnel because they were the gold, silver, and bronze medal winners.

Ten minutes had passed, and there was discussion as to who was going to issue them their medals. The officials didn't know if it would be Avery Brundage, the International Olympic Committee President, or Douglas Roby, the President of the U.S. Olympic Committee. Neither was chosen because of their unpopularity with the athletes. A committee member that was unknown to most of the athletes was chosen to issue the medals. The officials gave them directions as to how they were going to proceed to the victory stand. They told them the order in which each category would be called, and they lined up accordingly. After everything was arranged, John and Tommy began to have discussions as to what they had to wear to make a statement on the victory stand. John had some black love beads and a black shirt that he had borrowed from someone, and Tommy was to bring the pair of black gloves that his wife Denise purchased for him. When Tommy pulled the gloves out of his bag John came up with an idea as to how they were going to use them. He suggested to Tommy that each one of them could take a glove and give a demonstration of a clenched fist raised in the air. Tommy pondered for a quick second, and he said that the idea sounded cool. So John told Tommy that he should have first choice in terms of which glove he wanted to wear. Tommy chose the right hand glove, leaving John with the left. They placed the gloves in their pants until the appropriate time to put them on. There was no conversation as to how each of them would raise their hand. It was an individual thing. The black glove was to let the world know that they were representing the black race. They were representing the United States of America too, but particularly the black race.

John had a few more ideas that he shared with Tommy. He suggested that they roll their sweat pants up, showing their black socks. He said that the black socks would symbolize poverty in America and their stand against it. Further, he mentioned the fact that Puma had been providing them with all of their running equipment so it would be proper to place their Pumas on the stand. The conversation took them about fifteen minutes of discussion time, and what they were going to wear and do was finalized. Peter Norman was right next to Tommy and John while this discussion was going on. But they didn't know if Peter understood what their discussion was all about. So John asked Peter if he believed in human rights; he immediately responded with a "Yes." John, pleased with his response, asked him if he would be willing to wear an Olympian Project for Human Rights button. He again said, "Yes." The all-white Harvard Rowing Crew was favored to win a medal, and they were actively involved with the Olympic Project For Human Rights. They even passed out Human Rights buttons. Paul Hoffman, the captain of the Harvard Crew, and crew members: Scott Stekette, Curtis Canning, David Higgins, J. Cleave Livingston, and Andrew Larkin had written letters to the Olympic Committee to create dialogue to help the black athletes. They also had solicited other Olympic athletes to get involved with the movement despite opposition from their peers. John said that they were courageous.

John walked over to one of the Harvard crew guys and asked him for a button. He didn't have one but he felt compelled to give John the button that he was wearing. John carried the button to Peter who, without hesitation, pinned it on the left side of his chest. When Peter placed the button on his chest, it gave Tommy and John a great boost to see a man who is white take a stand. John stated that he has great respect for Peter because on that day he proved to him that he was his own man.

Coach Wright became extremely nervous because he got wind that Tommy and John were going to put on some sort of demonstration. So he went over to the ABC camera crew and told them that something negative was about to happen. He did not know what it was, but his main concern was that they not film the ceremony for the medal presentations. Stan had a lot of nerve asking the ABC crew to not film. The ABC crew was there to film everything that took place in the Olympics, and in essence, their response was, "Hey, this is history, and we are going to film it."

The time had come for the track and field Olympians to get into formation to march to the victory stand. Music was playing, the fans were cheering and screaming, the cameras were rolling, the photographers were snapping pictures, the recipients of the medals were anxiously awaiting the moment of glory to stand and be honored, their parents, friends and loved ones yelling and screaming their names. There was joy and jubilation throughout the stadium. While all of this was going on, John said that he had a quiet conversation with Tommy. He reminded Tommy that both of them had received hate letters, they had seen the mass murder perpetrated by the Mexican Army, they had been threatened with death by FBI and CIA agents, and some of the letters that they received threatened their lives. While pondering these things, John said these words to Tommy: "Tommy, you know what the sound of a gun sounds like, don't you?" He answered, "yes." John said, "Well, while the national anthem is being played, and we are standing on the victory stand with our fists raised in the air, the people will be shocked to silence and we should be able to hear the clicking of a gun." Tommy listened attentively and John continued, "So be listening for the sound and be ready to protect yourself by hitting the ground if you hear it." Tommy understood what John was saying, and he responded with a serious expression, saying, "OK, Los."

The Olympians marched out to the stand, and the medal ceremony began. Both John and Tommy put their black gloves on while they waited. When their places were called, the recipients walked up to the victory stand to receive their medals. Tommy and John walked up there with both hands behind them carrying their running shoes. Tommy's name was called first; he received the gold medal. He walked up to the official and he placed the medal over his head as he kneeled his 6'4" frame down to receive it. He was also given a box with an Olympic wreath in it. He stood up and placed his running shoes on the victory stand; then he stepped up on the victory stand raising both fists in the air due to the excitement. Peter Norman's name was called next, and he walked up, kneeled, and placed himself in front of Tommy as the silver medal winner. Lastly, John's name was called, and he walked up and kneeled to receive the bronze medal. But before he mounted the victory stand, he put his Puma running shoes on it. Tommy and John were standing on the victory stand in their black socks, and no one asked any questions about it. By now the black glove that Tommy wore had been detected because he had raised both hands in the air, forgetting that he had a glove on. John had stood there in the open with both hands behind him holding his shoes. No one in the stadium or in the world knew what the plan was with the gloves except John Carlos and Tommy Smith.

The people were cheering excitedly for them. The announcer for the public address system was the only thing that calmed them down. He asked that all please rise for the playing of America's National Anthem. The American flag stood tall, waving in Mexico City's thin air, and the entire stadium rose to their feet. In the meantime, Tommy, Peter, and John had to turn in another direction to face the flag. And without further ado, the playing of the National Anthem began. At the sound of the first trumpet, Tommy and John raised their fists and bowed their heads at about the same time. The majority of the people were focused on the flag, but finally it seemed that the entire stadium, the photographers, the cameras, the officials, and the Olympians focused their attention on them. Now the whole world was focused on them: standing tall, saying to America that they defied her hypocrisy, economic racism, and the way she treats people of color. As John later put it, "The American people in the stands were shocked into silence. One could hear a frog piss on cotton it was so quiet in the stadium."

This protest shocked the world. It reached heaven! God looked down on America that day saying that this hour has been ordained by Him, that He has used these men as His instruments to tell the world in a silent protest about America's wrong against all children who should be free.

I am free! I emphatically state that I was the most relaxed person in the stadium despite the fact that me and Tommy were facing death, ostracizing, economic death row, and a name that would spell disaster for anyone who wanted to be associated with it. I was standing there thinking about the prophetic vision of the protest that the Lord showed me when I was 7 years old. At the same time, I was reflecting back on my life, and everything that I had done up to that moment. The last thing that I thought about was the fact that out of the five billion people on the planet, Tommy, and I were selected by God to do a silent protest in front of the world. I was at peace in the middle of America's nightmare. I was ready to die!

When John and Tommy walked back to the tunnel in the stadium the world press was all over them, asking questions. Many fans were booing loudly, giving them the middle finger. Some made ugly faces, cursing and swearing at them, but some cheered! Tommy threw his fist up in the air again. This really pissed some people off, and they booed louder. Then John's fist went up. The reporters were so concentrated around them that

John told them to get the fuck back out of the way or he was going to kick some ass. His statement offended some reporters; however they still pressed them with questions.

After the protest, when John and Bob returned to Mel's villa they found all of their belongings sitting in front of the gate. Mel's wife had placed them there because she was disappointed about what John and Tommy had done. She actually waited for them to return, telling John that she did not like what they had done, and they were not welcome in her villa. That night they didn't get a chance to talk to Mel about the situation, but the Puma Shoe Company came to Tommy and John's rescue by arranging for them and their wives to stay in the downtown Hotel Diplomatica where the press and Olympic officials stayed.

The next morning the International Olympic Committee and Avery Brundage exploded with anger--the U.S. Olympics had better do something or he would see to it that the U.S. track team were disqualified. The U.S. Olympic Committee met and decided that they would suspend the two from the Olympic Village and send them home. The committee also agreed that it was of the utmost importance to bring in a black icon to talk to the black athletes about being patriotic to their country and the Olympics. There was one name that stood alone and that was the one and only Jesse Owens who had won four gold medals in the 1936 Berlin Olympics. Jesse was recruited by the Olympic Committee to speak to the black athletes. A meeting was set, and Jesse spoke.

It is rather ironic that after the Silent Protest Jesse Owens would be an advocate for the Olympic Committee. He had raised money for them on many occasions and spoke out in their behalf. It is a standard practice for white people to bring a good old Uncle Tom Negro in to speak against those of us who are willing to take a stand against racism and economic depression. At that time, Jesse could not see that the 1936 Olympics was one of the most social and political Olympics in the modern era. Further, he was unable to relate it to what was going on during the sixties. When Jesse had returned home from Germany, he did not get a thing except degradation and hardship. None of us listened to what Jesse had to say because he was out of date and out of touch with the real issues involved. We had to take a stand!

John and Tommy were informed that they were to leave the Olympic Village. John wasn't living in the Olympic Village, but Tommy was. John and Tommy's response to the order was that they didn't have to leave Mexico, and they had every right to remain there just like other U.S. citizens. Tommy left the village, but he and John remained in Mexico and watched the rest of the Olympic games. As far as the medals were concerned, their medals still counted as a victory for America. John and Tommy still have their Olympic Medals. They were not disqualified from the team; they were only kicked out of the Olympic Village and Mexico.

Very shortly, the world press contacted John and Tommy to see if they could do an interview, which they agreed to. But John told them that it had to be done in his room at the hotel. That afternoon the press filled the room to capacity. Camera crews, photographers, journalists,

FBI, CIA, Olympic Officials were there to vie for position to hear John and Tommy's views about the protest. There was camera on top of camera and one could hear the cameramen grunting, talking to each other about spacing, and what was about to happen in the interview. Everyone got situated, and the interview began with John and Tommy standing ready to answer questions about the protest. John said that the attitude of the press was very interesting because they came from many parts of the world, and their perceptions were different based on where they were from. John said that the press from third world countries was sympathetic to their cause because blacks and people of color lived there. On the other hand, the press from the Western world like the USA, England, Australia, South Africa, and other places that were run by whites, were opposed to the protest. Thus, the press was split in their ideas about the protest.

The press asked John and Tommy many questions: What was the purpose of making a protest statement during the Olympics? What was the psychology behind it? Why was the protest so extreme? Are you black Panthers? Why was protest necessary in the first place? Who orchestrated the protest? What was the significance of the black gloves, and black socks? Was the protest geared towards political prisoners like Nelson Mandela in South Africa, and blacks in other countries who fought against white power establishments like in India, Cuba, and other countries? Did someone pay you to protest? These were the types of questions that John and Tommy had to answer during the press conference. The press spent well over two hours asking questions: The responses were carried in every major newspaper and magazine in the world.

Bob Beamon had to jump in the finals on the day that John and Tommy had their interview with the press. John wondered how well he would perform under the difficult circumstances that the Silent Protest brought about. When it came time for Bob to jump, John was in the stadium telling everyone that Bob was going to do something special. The sun hadn't shone all day, but when it came time for Bob to jump, the sun broke through the clouds and shone a bright light on him. Bob took off down the runway with tremendous speed and perfect form. He approached the board very relaxed as he ran. But when he went to jump, he took off in the air with a force that took him where no man had gone.

All you could hear was ooh! Bob knew that he had jumped the best jump of his life. He was totally elated, but he did not know just how far he had jumped. The official tape measurer was standing looking at the place where he had jumped. He had to call for a different tape because the official one was not long enough. The tape was brought over and the official stood there for about two minutes just looking. Finally the officials measured the jump. All measurements were recorded using the metric system. The officials measured Bob's jump at 8 meters 90. They posted on the screen, and the fans went wild. Bob did not know how far that was in feet so he went over to Ralph Boston, asked him how far his jump was in feet. Ralph made the calculation: 29 1/2 feet. When Ralph told Bob the great news of his jump, Bob collapsed. He set a new world's record that lasted over 20 years.

John said that he was very happy for Bob because he was his friend and he had been instrumental in training him to compete at his greatest potential for those

211

30 days. When the world press, the Olympic officials, and others asked him how he did it, he said, "John Carlos trained me." One Olympic member's response was, "Don't ever mention that name." Bob's response was positive, but he never again mentioned to the press how John trained him to become a winner. John said that Bob wasn't man enough to stand up and speak the truth about how he trained him. He further stated that he would have never won a gold medal and set a new world's record had it not been for his special training services. John was really hurt by Bob's decision to forget about him. The Olympics ended with the closing ceremony on the 26th of October.

8

NCAA Championship

Championship Days

John had two months to prepare to attend San Jose State's 1968-69 spring semester to participate in track and field in January. He decided to leave Mexico and fly to Los Angeles to board another plane to return to San Jose. Upon his arrival in LA, the press got wind of his flight and flooded the airport to obtain as much information about the Silent Protest as possible. The airport personnel felt that they could save the general public some discomfort by allowing the reporters to do the interviews on the landing field. Tommy and John were together that day, and when they got off the plane, the reporters swarmed them with questions.

I definitely remember the sports reporter Brad Pie Junior from LA's famous radio station KGFJ, the station that played all of the Motown Sounds. There were other blacks from the press saying, "Hey, man, give me the scoop because I'm a brother." I did not pay that any mind because I was going to tell the truth about what I was feeling at the time anyway. So the brother thing wasn't necessary. Tommy and I answered several questions, and we did not have much time to answer them all because we were on airport time. So after we completed the interviews, they ushered us into a limousine to board the next plane to San Jose. Our flight took no longer than an hour to complete, and we landed in San Jose's Airport. There were several reporters wanting to do interviews, but not as many as in Los Angeles. The reporters and the passengers were there to either tell us about how good they felt about what we had done or tell us how they did not appreciate our exploits. It was a long day, and finally I got home to my family and friends.

When John arrived at his house on Reed Street, he saw that his neighbors (two white men) had made a large banner and spread it across John's house: "Welcome Home, John Carlos, Our Hero." John said that it really made him feel good inside because prior to that time most of white America had a negative attitude about the protest. So to see two young white men saying that he made an impact on them was good. They knew his character, and they expressed their sentiment in the banner. During those two months, John continued to train and hustle money to take care of his family.

The track season began with invitational meets where the best athletes in the nation and the world competed. The NCAA invitational issued medals to the winners whereas the AAU sponsors and promoters gave prizes like computers, typewriters, luggage, and other goods. John's attitude about the medals versus the prizes was that he was going to compete in the AAU invitational and earn prizes in spite of what the NCAA had to say about the situation. The NCAA committee tried to stop the AAU from issuing prizes to the athletes by using the amateur status rule, which indicated that the athlete could not earn money or prizes while amateurs. Losing amateur status would prevent the athlete from competing in college under a scholarship. So the athletes were in between in the conflict.

John had been invited to the Women's National Indoor Competition in Dayton, Ohio, to help the female athletes build their program. At that time, female athletes were not in the limelight. The TV stations would not broadcast the women's track and field events on TV; they would possibly give them some TV time if they had some track and field men running during their meets. John was the biggest name in track and field, and he wanted to use his name along with others to obtain TV time. He said that it was a shame that the women athletes weren't taken seriously because he said they were totally awesome. They inspired him! He felt very strongly about assisting them, and he wasn't going to allow anyone to stop him from participating in the track meet. The NCAA knew about the championship meet, and they issued a telegram to the athletes that were invited, telling them that they would strip them of their amateur status if they participated in the track meet. John told the NCAA, the press, and all of the athletes that received a telegram, that he did not care what the NCAA stated, he said that he was going to participate in the meet. The NCAA had their agenda and John had his. He knew that he was bread and butter for both associations, and it did not make any difference to him what they said. John ran in the meet and the TV stations filmed it, but they only showed the men. Nothing was done to those who participated.

John agreed that black communities all across America should come together and form a Black Athletic Association. The association would set down specific guidelines or rules to ensure that the black athlete receives the best possible scenario from any college or university they choose to attend. The rules would state specifically that no university would be able to exploit them for their athleticism. The university will also hire black mentors, from faculty to student tutors, to assist them. These rules along with others will ensure that the black athlete will have legal representation that is in the best interest for him or her, not the university. The university will get theirs from ticket sales, TV rights, paraphernalia, shoe endorsements, and other perks.

In the academic year of 1968-69, John had a major goal: to establish himself as the "Independent Sprint Champion of the World." He felt that he had to accomplish this goal because he had sacrificed races at the Olympic games. He said that he had in his mind to defeat all of his opponents unmercifully. He said that he was going to whup them over and over again, and he made this comment: "Yes, I did not win the gold medal in the 200-meter, nor did I run in the 100-meter in the Olympics, but I am going to show all of my opponents, the IOC, NCAA, and the world that John Carlos is the Mohammed Ali of track and field." John set his goal and challenged anyone who wanted to meet him on the track. He set the pace to dominate the 100-meter and the 200-meter that year. And he told the President of San Jose State University, Robert Clark, Bud Winters, his friends, and family before the track season began in 1968 that he was going to win the NCAA National Championship single handed. He was on a mission to shake the very foundations of track and field, and he drew strength every day thinking about it.

Establishing the title of Independent Champion Sprinter of the World was a force that kept him focused away from the negative and hostile environment that the Silent Protest in Mexico brought to his family, Tommy, and himself. From the time that he and Tommy raised their fists they became enemies of the United States Government and the FBI. Everywhere he went from that time on, there were agents from the FBI following him. He had a wife and child that he had to support, and America had closed the economic doors to him. He had been accustomed to being around his peers who were of celebrity status, and over-night 99% of them walked out of his life because they knew that to be associated with him could mean trouble for their careers. He had to think about the situation very carefully because he said that he would have died for some of them. But at the same time, they would have died economically had they continued to associate with him. So he forgave them, and he understood where they were coming from.

The NCAA Division I Track and Field Indoor Season began January 4, 1969, with an invitational meet in Washington DC. There was talk in the track and field world amongst the sprinters. It was said that there was not a tall sprinter alive who could defeat a short sprinter in the 60-yard dash. The talk got around to John, and he challenged all comers saying that he could defeat them all. John ran the 60-yard dash at the Washington meet, and he broke the world, national, and collegiate record by running 60 yards in 5.9 seconds. The record still stands!

The indoor season was a warm-up for John and a thriller for the track and field world. He performed some amazing feats. In the 100-yard dash, he did not run any time more than 9.3 seconds. He defeated everyone that came his way. In the 220-yard dash, he ran between a 20.7 and 20.2. Meanwhile, Lee Evans, Larry Walls, Ronnie Ray Smith, Neville Peyton, Sam Davies, and Jack Malloy dominated the 440 and the mile relay. By the time the indoor track season ended March 15, 1969, with the Indoor Nationals, San Jose State was ranked number one in the world.

John did not have an interest in earning a college degree. He wanted to attend San Jose State University to fulfill his promise to Coach Bud that he would run for him for one year in order to win the NCAA track and field championship. Although John did not have an interest in earning a degree, this does not mean that he was not interested in learning. Education isn't only found in books. It is found in experiencing different challenges in life, and gathering knowledge from those who are around you. John has been around some of the most influential people in the world, and colleges and universities don't want to acknowledge the fact that he learned more than most of their bachelor or master's degree graduates will ever learn. He obtained his education from his involvement with presidents of countries, kings and queens, governors, mayors and councilman from New York to LA, activists like Dr. Martin L. King, Dr. Harry Edwards, Stokely Carmichael, and H. Rap Brown, athletes from professional basketball, baseball, football, golf, and other sports, celebrities from TV, movies, singers, actors, heads of states, diplomats, famous college professors, commissioners of professional sports, curators of museums, artists, musicians, dancers, and most important-antly the everyday people whom he loved. And what's more, he has been on every continent in the world except Antarctica. He was recognized not only as a runner; he was acknowledged as a man with dignity and courage to fight for what was right. What the students were learning in books, John experienced directly. European art, history, music, folklore, dance, monuments, museums, you name it; he had been there and done that. John said that he could say the same for Australia, Africa, the Middle East, the Caribbean, Mexico, America, Canada, South America, and other places.

The knowledge that he obtained could not be put in the context of a degree. Many college and university graduates have never been out of the country, and many will never have the opportunity to get themselves in the kind of social arena that he was privileged to. You will find many people in the military, entertainment, and politics who bragged about their exploits traveling around the world; many have said that world travel distinguished them from those who have earned an education and hadn't traveled. Universities and colleges should recognize this most excellent way of obtaining an education and prepare a way to allow people like John to challenge institutions in order to earn a degree.

During the first part of the spring semester, several universities across the country contacted John. They wanted him to talk to the student population about racism in America and how to combat it. John spoke at Hayward State, Howard University, Kent State, University of Washington, Colombia University, San Jose State University, Sac State, Oberland College, Virginia State, University of Tennessee, Knoxville College, Central State Ohio, University of Southern California and other schools. He talked to students all across this great United States although he had no formal education, no degree, and no prior oratory skills.

The Outdoor season began March 22, 1969 with the University of Washington. John ran 9.3 seconds in the hundred. He ran the 440 relay with Sam Davies, Kirk, Clayton, Ronnie, and Ray Smith. They ran 39.6 seconds, taking first place. San Jose State defeated Stanford, Arizona State in the 100, 220, and the 440 relays. They also dominated these races in the All Comers Meet, and the Dogwood Relays in Knoxville, Tennessee.

John had something to prove at the Mount Sac Relays in Walnut, California, April 26, 1969. Hue Malodge, the Mt. Sac. Track coach, had been on the '68 Olympic Committee. He was the one who determined who would run in a particular event during the Olympic trials. And John believed that it was he who conspired with Stan Wright, the Olympic sprint coach, to disallow him to run the 100-meter race in Olympic Trials in Echo Summit. John had won all the heats in the 100-meter during the preliminaries, and when it came time to run in the Trials, he was disallowed because he had not run the 100-meter prior to the preliminary trials due to an injury that he suffered in Trinidad. Running the 100-meter would have qualified John to run the mile relay, which would have given him a chance to win a gold in the 100-meter, 200-meter, and the mile relay. John did not hold a grudge against Malodge, and forgave him.

John wanted to show Coach Malodge that he was a good sport, and he was going to give the people a show. So he ran extremely well in the 100-meter and again he raised his hands in the air at the victory line. His time was a 9.2. Coach Bud was running around jumping up and down saying how happy he was that John ran such a fast time. Then he thought about the situation and he said that John could have broken the world's record had he not thrown his hands in the air. So he was happy and sad at the same time. John knew that he could have broken the world record, but he did not want to do it in front of that particular crowd. He was saving it as a gift for his people (blacks) at the Fresno Relays.

With his desire to show his dominance in track and field, he had an opponent to take care of, and that was Charlie Green from Nebraska St. University. He got his chance at the San Jose Invitational May 3, 1969. San Jose State invited Charlie Green, one of the top runners in the country, down from Nebraska St. University to run against them in the hundred yard dash. John ran a 9.2 in the hundred yard dash at that meet, and the "Track and Field News" captured that moment with a photo of him running with his hands held high at the victory line. Charlie Green was his first big heavyweight fight of the season.

The West Coast Relays in Fresno, California, May 10, 1969, was like no other relay of its kind. Its uniqueness was based on the fact that the majority of the people that attended it were black people. I am talking 90% black. Every black fraternity and sorority in the state, and many from other parts of the country, attended. The hotels, supermarkets, restaurants, gas stations, and practically all businesses earned money from the event.

A day before the event, you would see hundreds and hundreds of cars coming from all directions to the Fresno Relays. It was like a carnival. Women would prepare a year in advance just to get a glimpse of the brothers on the track team. These fine black women were serious about being with a black man. They brought food and drinks of every kind. And they would fix themselves up to the max, outfitted each day with new clothes. They were also prepared to party all night long. They missed classes, tests, jobs, church, study, and everything because, while the relays were going on, nothing else mattered.

They were totally committed to make sure the brothers were well taken care of from the beginning to the end of the event. John said that these girls were not tramps but were sophisticated sisters with education and skills. The kind of women that a man would take home to mama. John had much love for the black sisters!

Being from Harlem, heart of the black Renaissance, John was accustomed to being around places where the people get down having fun. So he enjoyed himself to the max by mingling with the fans before he ran in a race. He was focused, and he wanted to give the people a race that they would never forget. On this day he was there to show his people who the real champion of track and field was, and the people had a feeling that something special was about to happen. It was in the air! He said that the powers of light were shining down upon him and he felt so good from being around his people that he could hardly contain himself. John was trying to talk to everybody there. He wanted them to know that he was one of them. He wanted them to know that only God was to be reverenced, and John was only His son utilizing the gifts that He gave him to run. That is the real reason why John was always in the stands with the people.

The weather that day was cold and dreary. As a matter of fact it rained. John left the stands and went down to the track, and he began to do his warm-up drills. He ran the race through his mind as he always did, but this time he ran it like never before. The race began when the officials summoned them to move into their blocks. John went through his usual ritual of talking to his opponents, and when he got himself set in the blocks, he shut everything down. He shut down the cheering, the external noise around him, the officials and everything else. He listened for the one thing that would set him off from the blocks and that was the voice that said, "Runners, on your marks, get set" -- Boom. The instant that John heard the gun, he broke forth from the blocks like a beam of light streaking across the heavens on a new moon's night. Nothing else was in sight but John. He streamed down the lane toward the finish line running above the ground. For on that day, he was on a different plane. There was no force on earth that could have caught up with him because the light that shined down on him was leading him. John became one with it and he felt a surge of energy that surpassed all of the training that he had ever done. It boosted John to a higher degree of consciousness and crowned him with the title the World's Fastest Man. It was not to be written and accepted by man, but the Lord God who ordained it. And on that day he ran faster than any man juiced (steroid user) or free (no steroids). John ran an 8.8 seconds in the 100-yard dash.

Man said that it was impossible to do. But the people were a witness unto God. The officials could not believe what they saw because they saw with their eyes and not with their hearts. They saw but did not see. They heard but did not accept the cheers of joy and elation that came from those who witnessed the gift. There were official and unofficial timers on the track and in the stands. Some had 8.7 sec. others had 8.8, 8.9 and 9.0 sec., but the official timer had no time because he was there with me. He could not believe what he saw, and by the time he came back down to the physical world he clocked me at 9.1 sec.

There was a meeting of the minds of the officials to see if anyone could come up with a solution to the problem. So in order to put the situation into their terms they allowed me to tie the world's record by taking an average time of the things that they did not want to see or believe. The world's record was 9.1 sec., and if one would take an average of the scores, he or she would have to calculate a score that is below 9.1 sec. To justify their rationale, they say that it was wind-aided. No wind in the world can make a man run 0.4 sec faster. On average the wind gives .01 or maybe .02 sec., and that is about all.

John was stripped of a world record in the Olympic trials because his shoes were illegal, and now he would be stripped of a world record because the official timer could not believe what he saw. There was not anyone within ten yards of him when he crossed the finish line, and the officials gave the other contenders a 9.3-sec. timing. John was robbed once again, but the official time will always stay with the people and God.

Tiff Milan, a triple jumper from UCLA, and presently a Hollywood producer, described the scene as a track and field carnival made in heaven. Also a track and field participant, Tiff witnessed John's 8.8 second hundred-yard run. He described it as something out of this world. He said that he has never seen or heard of anyone running that fast since that day, and the race was truly a gift to all those who observed it. The officials were the only ones who could not believe what they had seen, and disqualified John's new-world record time, giving him the current world record. If that 8.8 second hundred-yard time had been accepted, it would still be a world record to this day.

There were many colleges and universities that were jealous of San Jose State University's excellent NCAA Track and Field Team. Colleges and universities such as UCLA, USC, Oregon, and other powerhouse teams were not happy with the fact that a small school like San Jose State should be ranked number one in the world, so they avoided them during the regular season. John mentioned how San Jose State University invited UCLA and USC to run against them. They offered to assist in transportation, housing, and whatever they needed to bring the competition home. UCLA and USC refused the offer. John told them all: "You may avoid us now, but during championship time, you can't hide."

John had proved to be the best in the world in the 100-meter, 200-meter, and the sprint relays, and there were 5 more track meets before the 1969 NCAA Championship began. He ran in the Martin Luther King Games in Philadelphia, Pa., the Modesto Relays, Compton Invitational in Los Angeles, Ca., Orange County Invitational in Orange, Ca., and Hayward Invitational at Hayward, Ca. He continued to dominate each race, moving eagerly towards the goal that he had set to win the NCAA Division I Championship. John had no doubt in his mind that he was the best in the world, and he knew that without a doubt, he was going to win the championship.

The NCAA Championship began June 19th, ending on the 21st of June 1969. During the championship, the critics were saying that schools like Tennessee, USC, UCLA, and other powerhouse schools would sneak in and take points away from San Jose. It seems that the critics wanted any and everybody but San Jose State to win. San Jose State's coach, Bud Winters, had sent many athletes to the Olympics, and John said that it was rather ironic that such a great coach had not won a National Championship with all of the talent.

All of the colleges and universities that San Jose had invited to race were represented in the NCAA championships. John was ready to take them all on. There were several men who could run the 100-yard dash in less than 9.2 seconds. Here is a list of the men from different universities that ran in the NCAA Championship: Bill Hurd from Notre Dame, Willie Turner from Oregon State, Jerry Bright from Arizona State, Lennox Miller from USC, Reggie Robinson from UCLA, Rockie Woods from Texas A&M, and Mel Gray from Missouri. Ronnie Ray Smith, Kirk Clayton, and John Carlos represented San Jose State.

In the 100 heat John ran 9.3 seconds, placing first against Bill Hurd (NotreDame), and Willie Turner (Oregon) who placed second and third respectively. In the 100 Semifinal John ran 9.1 seconds, placing first against Lennox Miller (UCLA), and Ronnie Ray Smith (San Jose State) who placed second and third place. The 100 Final was a very close race. John defeated Lennox Miller (USC) by a tenth of a second while his teammate Ronnie Smith placed third. The 220 heat in the championship had some good competitors, but none of them came close to John's time. Ronnie Ray Smith, Willie Turner, Bill Hurd, Tom Randolf (Western Michigan), Mel Gray, Larry Shuerer (Washington St.), and Orin Richburg

(Kent St.) never ran faster than a 20.9 in the 220 heat, Semifinal, and the Final. John won the Final heat and tied the meet record with a 20.2 second run. In the 440 Relay heat John ran with Kirk Clayton, Sam Davis, and Ronnie R. Smith, setting a new American record, running 38.8 seconds in the 440. They ran the Final race, running the 440 in 39.1 seconds. Rice University came in second, and Texas A & M took third. Ultimately, San Jose won the NCAA Championship.

John said that winning the championship was not easy. For one thing, the weather was bad that day; it was raining. The officials gave San Jose State the worst lanes. As a matter of fact, when it came time to run the sprint relays, they gave them lane one. Lane one is always given to the person with the worst time. It was a known fact that they were going for the world's record, and placing them in lane one could affect their time. Further, lane one was filled with puddles of water three to six inches deep due to the fact that they had not set the track up correctly. San Jose protested about the water and the officials reluctantly swept the water off the track. The water continued to be a problem, but SJSU decided that they would run anyway. They won the race, only missing the world record by one tenth of a second. They felt very good about their time despite the inclement weather, and they proved the critics wrong by winning the 1969 NCAA Championship.

Winning a championship proved to be the highlight of Bud's career. And when it came time for John to back up his words to Bud, he did exactly what he said he would do. Out of the sixty points that were scored in the National Championship, John scored 35.

There was much celebration on the victory stand. John and his teammates had shocked the track and field world, proving everybody wrong. They were not only ranked nationally; they were ranked by some polls as being the number one track and field team in the world. Ronnie Smith, Kirk Clayton, Sam Davies, and all of the team were on the victory stand with the exception of one man, Larry Walls (hurdler). He refused to join them on the victory stand because the officials said he scratched during his race.

John looked at Larry, and he told him that he'd better get up on the platform. They were not concerned about the error that the officials made when they said that he scratched. Everyone on the team that watched the race closely knew that he did not scratch. The officials made a mistake. Further, Larry was an intricate part of the team, and he was instrumental in getting them to the championship. The team wanted him to share the victory with them, and eventually he joined them in their celebration.

When the 1969 NCAA Track and Field Champions returned to San Jose, the local newspaper had John Powell's name (discus thrower) as the one who won the championship for San Jose. John still feels today that the newspaper printed the article in Powell's favor because he was a flower child, and John was the controversial ghetto kid. Powell was a contributing factor, but he only scored three points. John scored 35 points. If anyone's name should have been on the front page, it should have been John Carlos' name.

One week after the NCAA Division I Championship, John found himself in Florida competing for the AAU Championship and the right to go to Europe and other parts of the world to compete. The actual date of the event was June 28, 1969. John had been dealing with a lot of negativity from the government, the athletic associations, the press, businesses, enemies, and his friends, based on what he did in Mexico. But despite all of the pressures, he was psyched up to break the world's record again in the 100-yard dash. The press, NCAA, AAU, all the track and field organizations, along with many citizens, felt that John was a militant, a demon, and a troublemaker, ready to create havoc and chaos.

When John arrived at the stadium, he noticed that the police had on riot gear. He wasn't thinking about anything other than breaking the world's record, but the authorities in Florida feared that he was going to somehow create a riot or something. He didn't allow any of that to deter him from focusing on what he had come there to do. He walked onto the field as if nothing had occurred, and he began to stretch and do his warm-up exercises. After he stretched, he jogged around the inside track to warm his muscles up. For some strange reason, the masses of people in the audience began to focus their attention on him. It was as if they had been put under a spell or some magical potion! They seemed to adore him the more they looked at him, and the admiration turned into an emotion and the only thing they could do was applaud him! Remember now, this is a Southern audience, and they could not help but respect him as a man even if they hated him for what he had done. The riot police and all of their plans to suppress what they thought would become a bad situation became a positive one. John was so elated that at one point he could not contain himself. All he could do was wave to the fans, and thank God that He walked into that place with him. He said that the people showed him a lot of love that day!

The love and admiration from the fans did not change the minds and hearts of the officials involved in running the track meet. When John ran the first heat, and the semi-heat, he took first place. Now to show you how political things can be, when it came time for him to run the final race, he was placed in the outside lane. Normally when an athlete wins all of their heats, the officials place them in the center lane of the track. John had won all of his heats, but due to the controversy in Mexico, he received the worst lane on the track. The final race was about to begin and the official said in a whispering tone, "On your mark, get set." John couldn't hear, so he raised his hand and said, "I can't hear you." Everyone got up and reset. The official began again to get them started, this time his voice was even lower. In addition to his low voice, a plane flew over, and at the same time something special happened at another event that created a noisy response from the audience. While all of this was going on, the official shot the gun; everyone took off except John.

Willy Davenport, an Olympic hurdler, was standing behind John and he quickly stated, "If you want to go to Europe, you better hurry up and catch these guys." When John looked up, all he could see were asses shimmying. Everything was moving in nanoseconds. He heard the gun, Willie's voice, and in his mind he said, "I have to place to go to Europe. So I hit it into high gear and I ran all of them down. Through sheer determination and the power to turn the juice on at the right time, I won the race." But before he could place one foot over the finish line, the announcer stated that a sprinter by the name of Ivory Crockett was the winner. John knew that he had won the race and he knew that the videotape would prove that he did. When the tape was reviewed, it proved that he had won. John said that it seemed that the race was programmed for him to lose, but through God and determination he prevailed.

John had earned his opportunity to travel to Europe and around the world to compete. The first competition took place in Hawaii, and from there he returned to Los Angeles to the USA-USSR-Commonwealth Meet. He took first place in both meets. Europe would be the next stop. He competed in Malmo, Sweden and in Stuttgart and Augsburg, West Germany. He ran extremely well in all of his meets, taking firsts in all of them. In Europe, track and field athletes are almost worshipped. When an athlete wins a big event, it is on the front page. The Germans loved John Carlos. After leaving Germany he returned to South Lake Tahoe to compete in the Indian Summer Games. He dominated the games, taking first again.

John had won the 1969 NCAA Championship; he ran track around the world for the AAU. Before long, he felt that there were no further challenges for him in track and field. He needed finances to feed his family, and a new family member, his first son, Malik Carlos, who was born March 5, 1970. John, having a son to carry on the Carlos name, was a very proud dad.

John's 1969 Track And Field Season Championship

January 4 - Washington CYO, Washington, D.C.
60 yd. dash – 1st, John Carlos, 5.9 (world record, American record, collegiate record).
January 17 - Los Angeles Invitational, Los Angeles, Calif.
60 yd. dash. – 1st, John Carlos, 6.1.
January 25 - Seattle Invitational, Seattle, Washington
60 yd. dash – 1st., John Carlos, 6.2.
February 14 - Maple Leaf Games, Toronto, Ontario
*50 yd. dash – 1st, John Carlos, 5.3.
*300 yd. dash – 2nd, John Carlos, 31.6.
February 15 - Herald Examiner Invitational, Los Angeles, Calif.
*60 yd. dash –2nd, John Carlos, 6.1.
*Mile Relay - 1st, San Jose State (Larry Walls, Jack Malloy, John Carlos, Lee Evans), 3:18.8
March 8 - SJSU vs. Athens Athletic Club, Sacramento State, Cal State Hayward
*100 yd. dash - 1st, John Carlos, 9.4. 2, Ronnie Ray Smith (SJSU), 9.4 3, Byron Wilson (SJSU), 9.9. 4, Reggie Pruitt (Athens), 21.8.

*220 yd. dash - 1st, John Carlos, 20.3 (w). 2,
Ronnie Ray Smith (SJSU), 20.9. 3, Sam Davis
(SJSU), 21.6. 4, Reggie Pruitt (Athens), 21.8.
*Mile Relay - 1st, San Jose State (Larry Walls,
Neville Myton, John Carlos, Lee Evans), 3:14.6.
2, Cal State Hayward, 3:22.4. 3, Sacramento
State, 3:23.4.

March 14-15 - NCAA Indoor Championships, Detroit Mich.
60 yd. dash - 1st, John Carlos, 6.0.

March 22   SJSU vs. Washington
*440 Relay - 1st, San Jose State (Sam Davis, Kirk
Clayton, Ronnie Ray Smith, John Carlos), 39.6.
*100 yd. dash - 1st, John Carlos, 9.3 (w). 2, Sam
Davis (SJSU), 9.7 (w). 3, Kirk Clayton (SJSU),
10.1 (w).
*220 yd. dash - 1st, John Carlos, 22.7. (w). 2, Ben
Johnson (UW), 22.1 (w).

March 29   SJSU vs. Stanford
*440 Relay - 1st, San Jose State (Byron Wilson,
Lee Evans, Ronnie Ray Smith , John Carlos), 40.6.
Stanford disqualified.
*100 yd. dash - 1st, John Carlos, 9.3 (w). 2,
Ronnie Ray Smith (SJSU), 9.5. 3, Fred Storck
(Stan), 9.7.
*220 yd. dash - 1st, John Carlos, 20.4. 2, Fred
Storck (Stan), 22.3, Byron Wilson (SJSU), 22.3.

April 5   <u>**SJSU vs. Arizona State**</u>

*440 Relay - 1st, San Jose State (Sam Davis, Lee Evans, Ronnie Ray Smith , John Carlos), 40.5. 2, Arizona State (Fair Hooker, Quill Nebeker, John Holbrook, Jerry Bright), 49.4.
*100 yd. dash - 1st, John Carlos, 9.3 (w). 2, Ronnie Ray Smith (SJSU), 9.6. 3, Jerry Bright (ASU), 9.7.
*220 yd. dash - 1st, John Carlos, 21.4. 2, Jerry Bright (ASU), 21.7. 3, Sam Davis (SJSU), 22.2.

April 12   <u>**All-comers Meet**</u>

*440 Relay - 1st, San Jose State (Sam Davis, Lee Evans, Ronnie Ray Smith, John Carlos), 41.2
*100 yd. dash - 1st, John Carlos, 9.3 (w). 2, Ronnie Ray Smith (SJSU), 9.5. 3, Bill Edmondson, 9.6.

April 19   <u>**Dog Wood Relays -**</u>
<u>**Knoxville, Tennessee**</u>
*440 Relay - 1st, San Jose State (Sam Davis, Kirk Clayton, Ronnie Ray Smith, John Carlos), 39.5.
*880 Relay - 1st, San Jose State (Sam Davis, Lee Evans, Ronnie Ray Smith , John Carlos), 1:22.7.
*100 yd. dash - 1st, John Carlos, 9.5.
*220 yd. dash - 1st, John Carlos, 22.0.

SANTA CLARA
YOUTH VILLAGE

April 26   **Mt. Sac Relays -**
Walnut, Calif.
*440 Relay - 1st, San Jose State (Sam Davis, Lee
Evans, Ronnie Ray Smith, John Carlos), 39.6.
*880 Relay - 1st, San Jose State (Sam Davis, Lee
Evans, Ronnie Ray Smith, John Carlos), 1:22.7.
*100 yd. dash - 1st, John Carlos, 9.2.

May 3   **San Jose State Invitational**
*100 yd. dash - 1st, John Carlos, 9.0 (w). 2,
Ronnie Ray Smith (SJSU), 9.3 (w). 3, Billy Gaines
(Un), 9.3; 4, Charlie Greene (Un), 9.3.
*220 yd. dash - 1st, John Carlos, 20.5 (w). 2, Lee
Evans (SJSU), 20.7 (w). 3, Jerry Williams (AAC),
20.7 (w).

May 10   **West Coast Relays - Fresno, Calif.**
*440 Relay - 1st, San Jose State (Sam Davis, Lee
Evans, Ronnie Ray Smith, John Carlos), 39.7.
*880 Relay - 1st, San Jose State (Sam Davis, Lee
Evans, Ronnie Ray Smith, John Carlos), 1:22.3.
*100 yd. dash - 1st, John Carlos, 9.1.

May 18   **Martin Luther King Games -**
Philadelphia, Pa.

*440 Relay - 1st, San Jose State (Sam Davis, Lee Evans, Ronnie Ray Smith, John Carlos), 40.3
*100 meters- 2nd, John Carlos, 10.1.

May 24   Modesto Relays - Modesto, Calif.
*440 Relay - 1st, San Jose State (Sam Davis, Lee Evans, Ronnie Ray Smith, John Carlos), 39.7.
*100 meters- 2nd, John Carlos, 10.1.
*220 yd. dash – 2nd John Carlos, 20.4 (w).

June 7   Compton Invitational - Los Angeles, Calif.
*100 yd. dash - 1st, John Carlos, 9.5.
*220 yd. dash – 2nd John Carlos, 20.7.

June 14   Orange County Invitational - Orange, Calif.
*100 yd. dash - 1st, John Carlos, 9.5.
*220 yd. dash – 2nd, John Carlos, 21.0.

June 15   Hayward Invitational - Hayward, Calif.
*100 yd. dash - 1st, John Carlos, 9.5.
*220 yd. dash – 2nd, John Carlos, 20.8. 2, Lee Evans (SJSU), 21.0.

June 19 - 21   NCAA Championships - Knoxville, Tenn.

100 Heat - 1st, John Carlos, 9.3. 2, Bill Hurd (Notre Dame), 9.4. 3, Willie Turner (Oregon State), 9.6. Also, Jerry Bright (Arizona State), 9.7, Dave Masters (California), 9.8, Scott Hendricks (Texas A&M), 9.8, Bob Wilson (Pacific), 9.8.

100 Semifinal - 1st, John Carlos, 9.1. 2, Lennox Miller (USC), 9.3. 3, Ronnie Ray Smith (SJSU), 9.3. 4, Rockie Woods (Texas A&M), 9.3. Also, Reggie Robinson (UCLA), 9.3, Willie Turner (Oregon State), 9.3, Tom Randolph (Western Michigan), 9.6. All times wind-aided.

100 Final - 1st, John Carlos, 9.1. 2, Lennox Miller (USC), 9.2. 3, Ronnie Ray Smith (SJSU), 9.3. 4, Mel Gray (Missouri), 9.3. 5, Bill Hurd (Notre Dame), 9.4 6, Reggie Robinson (UCLA), 9.4. Also Larry Highbaugh (Indiana), 9.5, Kirk Clayton (SJSU), 9.5. All times wind-aided.

220 Heat - 1st, John Carlos, 20.4. 2, Larry Scheurer (Washingtion State), 21.0. 3, Orin Richburg (Kent State), 21.1. Also Clifton Forbes (Nebraska), 21.1, Rich Coulter (USC), 21.2, Greg Marks (Oregon State), 21.7, Charles Rushing (Redlands), 21.8, Bob Wilson (Pacific, 22.0, John Hutcherson (Virginia Tech), no time.

<u>220 Semifinal</u> - 1st, John Carlos, 20.4. 2,Wayne Collett (UCLA), 21.0. 3, Mel Gray (Missouri), 20.9. 4, Larry Schuerer (Washington State), 21.0 Also, Ronnie Ray Smith (SJSU), 21.3., Roger Colglazier (Abilene Christian), 21.4, Julio Meade (Kansas), did not finish.

<u>220 Final</u> - 1st, John Carlos, 20.2 (ties meet record). 2, Tom Randolph (Western Michigan), 20.9. 3, Bill Hurd (Notre Dame), 20.9. 4, Wayne Collett (UCLA), 20.9. Also, Orin Richburg (Kent State), 20.9, Willie Turner (Oregon State), 21.7.

<u>440 Relay Heat</u> - 1st, San Jose State (Sam Davis, Kirk Clayton, Ronnie Ray Smith, John Carlos), 38.8 (new American record). 2, UCLA, 39.6. 3, Rice, 39.7. 4, Oregon State, 40.1. Also, Michigan, 40.5, Montana, 40.7, Mt. St. Mary's, 41.5, Pacific, no time, California, disqualified.

<u>440 Final</u> - 1st, San Jose State (Sam Davis, Kirk Clayton, Ronnie Ray Smith, John Carlos), 39.1. 2, Rice, 39.5. 3, Texas A&M, 39.5. 4, Kansas, 40.0. 5, Oregon State, 40.1. 6, Washington State, 40.1. Also, USC, disqualified, UCLA, disqualified.

June 28 - 29   National AAU Outdoor Championships - Miami, FL.
*100 yd. dash – 2nd, John Carlos, 9.3.
*220 yd. dash - 1st, John Carlos, 20.2.

July 12   **Hawaiian Invitational - Honolulu, Hawaii**
*100 yd. dash - 1st, John Carlos, 9.4.
*220 yd. dash - 1st, John Carlos, 21.3.

July 18 - 19   **U.S.A. - USSR - British Commonwealth Meet - Los Angeles, Calif.**
*100 meters - 1st, John Carlos, 10.3.
*200 meters – 2nd, John Carlos, 20.3.

July 24   **Malmo Invitational - Malmo, Sweden**
*100 meters - 1st, John Carlos, 10.3.
*200 meters - 1st, John Carlos, 21.0.

July 30 - 31   **Americas vs. Europe Dual Meet - Stuttgart, West Germany**
*100 meters - 1st, John Carlos, 10.2.
*200 meters - 1st, John Carlos, 20.4.

August 5 - 6   **U.S.A. vs. West Germany Dual Meet - Augsburg, West Germany**
*100 meters - 1st, John Carlos, 10.1.
*200 meters - 1st, John Carlos, 20.3.

September 12   **South Lake Tahoe Indian Summer Games - S. Lake Tahoe, Calif.**
*100 meters - 1st, John Carlos, 9.9 (w).
*200 meters - 1st, John Carlos, 20.2 2, Lee Evans (San Jose State), 20.4.

9

Pro-Football

Pro-football

In the 1969-70 pro-football season there was some talk about John becoming an NFL player. Through the press and some contacts, John received word that the NFL was interested in drafting him to play professional football. He knew that he had the athletic ability to play and excel in the game, but the only football that he had played was on the streets in Harlem's asphalt jungle. He had never played organized football.

The Dallas Cowboys, the Kansas City Chiefs, and the Philadelphia Eagles were all talking about drafting him. As far as contracts were concerned, the average football player was not earning the millions of dollars that professional ball players earn today, but one could earn a good living and live comfortably well. The salary base for a player like John was around 25 to 35 thousand dollars for a pro contract. The established super star players earned around 60 thousand. In those days the Canadian football league could compete with the NFL in all areas of recruitment and salaries. As a matter of fact, the Canadian Football League paid their players more than the National Football League. John's athletic ability, along with his world-class speed, made him an attractive commodity to both the NFL and the CFL even though it wasn't known whether or not he had the ability to play organized football. It was known that if he were to be used as a down field runner, there would be times that he would have to be double covered due to his great straight forward speed.

When the Dallas Cowboys contacted him about playing for them, he was very skeptical about returning to Texas due to the negative experience he had had at East Texas State. The Dallas management tried to convince him that he wouldn't have a problem there. They could not convince him about anything, and he chose to try out with the Philadelphia Eagles. Profootball for John meant one thing: he could feed his family. He could not find a job doing anything else, and sports were all that he knew.

When he arrived in Philadelphia, he said that he received some information that seemed like a conspiracy. He was informed that he was allowed to play football only to get him out of the amateur track and field arena. Once he signed professionally in football, he was no longer eligible to run as an amateur.

The Eagles management knew that John was a bona fide sprinter. They also knew that he had a name. So they signed him to a $25,000 a year contract. They also gave him a bonus for signing. John was very eager to play, and as you know by now, he was always in top form.

It was a rather unfortunate thing for football - and John - his NFL football career was cut short. In the first three weeks of the pre-season, he was injured in a freak accident. The Eagles' Franklin's Field was covered with Astro-Turf. It was a turf that John was not accustomed to running on. During training he ran curl patterns with Irv Cross, the defense back for Philadelphia. One day he and Irv were training and Irv threw the ball to John, and he planted his foot down onto the turf. The Astroturf locked his cleat solid. He reached for the ball, and he heard this popping sound in his leg. Hearing the sound didn't alarm him, he just kept running. But after a few more patterns it didn't feel right anymore. He continued practicing, but he knew that something was wrong.

He attended practice the next day, and his leg seemed to be dislocated. He asked the head coach Jerry Williams if he could see the doctor. The Eagles set up an appointment for him to visit Dr. Nixon, an orthopedic surgeon in Philadelphia. That same day he took a cab to Dr. Nixon's office where Lane Howl, a tight end, and others were waiting for the doctor to examine their knees. It wasn't very long before John was on the table being examined. The doctor began by turning his leg around and feeling it, then said, "We'll put you in tomorrow and we'll operate in the morning." Dr. Nixon said that John had torn a ligament in his right knee, and they would have to operate in order to repair it. John was shocked. This was his first year as a professional.

Jerry Williams, the Eagles coach, was very impressed with John's great speed. He made a comment to John saying that if he could learn to catch the ball, he could become a great football player. Before the injury Coach Williams stated that he was willing to take a chance with him. The chance would allow John to adjust to the game and the Eagles' system. Nonetheless, the Eagles coach would have to wait for the next season to see if he would still have the same speed after the operation.

The operation was difficult to accept. John had to adjust psychologically. It was the first time that he had ever been in the hospital since his birth. He had been the fastest man in the world for some time, and now they were going to be cutting his leg open to repair it.

The operation was a success. He knew that he had to rehabilitate himself and prove that he was still fast. There were football players on the team who thought they were faster than him, and he knew that he would be challenged as soon as he returned to camp.

The most difficult thing for him to deal with after the operation was the type of cast that they put on him. The doctor didn't place a traditional cast from the foot to the leg; he placed a cast on him from his foot to his waist. He could not bend his leg at all.

Everything that I tried to do was difficult. Eventually I got used to it and maneuvered myself to the point that I could get around without getting frustrated. I healed in about three to four months, and the doctor took the cast off. That was one of the happiest days in my life because I was not used to being confined. I knew that I had a rough road ahead of me in terms of getting myself back into world class condition. So I took it one day at a time and I began to rehabilitate myself for the next NFL season.

The Eagles had to pay John even though he was injured. Time passed quickly before next pre-season rolled around. John had trained himself back to damn near perfection. He ran at great speed despite his operation. So by the time the pre-season came around, he was in good running condition.

The Philadelphia Eagles had drafted a new recruit named Harold Carmichael. John said that he's the main reason that his pro career with the Eagles ended so abruptly. Harold was a trained football player who had all of the necessary skills to run and catch a football with great ability. He was a gifted athlete made for football,

John said. Harold could catch anything, but he was concerned with whether it would be him or John that would make the team. John said:

> Harold worried because he knew that I had a name and reputation in track and field. Carmichael had the ability to make great catches, yet I had the ability to run patterns with great speed. I told him that I would teach him how to run quicker and he said that he would help me with catching the ball.

During the Eagles' 1970-71 pre-season, time was not on John's side. They expected him to adjust to the system quickly. On top of that, John felt that the star quarterback, Norm Sleeve, did not like him. Norm was also a Southerner. John said, he never threw the ball so that John could catch it. It was always at his back, leg, knee, or his butt. Sometimes it wouldn't hit him at all. Coach Williams said that as long as the ball is near, he should be able to catch it. John began to realize that his lack of football experience was detrimental to his career. His heart was in it, but again time was not on his side.

There were many players on the Eagles that wanted John to succeed. They offered to assist him, but his ability to catch the football was poor. He soon found out about the politics in professional sports. He saw several good players get cut from the team for no apparent reason. Soon it would be his turn to get the call to the office for dismissal. Instead of giving the Eagles the pleasure of cutting him from the team, he told them that he was leaving. John figured that a short-lived career in football with the money that he had for signing would last until he was able to find a meaningful job. He had been with the Eagles for a little more than a year.

The next week John received a call from a guy named J.I. Albrecht, the General Manager and Director of Player Personnel for the Canadian Football League's Montreal Allouettes. J.I. had also been a scout for the San Francisco Forty Niners, Raiders, and other NFL teams. According to the rules and regulations of the Canadian football league, any athlete who had not played organized football at the grassroots level, high school, or college level qualified as being a non-import or Canadian. John, not having played football, qualified as an import or Canadian. The head football coach was Sam Etcheverry - better known as Sam "the rifle" Etcheverry. He had been a quarterback in the CFL, coming out of the University of Denver during the 1950's. The number-one quarterback for the Allouettes was a southerner from Virginia named Sonny Wade.

I interviewed J.I., and he was very open and honest about everything. He began the conversation telling me that everyone that was white in the camp had a negative attitude about John's Silent Protest in Mexico. But he was open to find out why he did it. Had he not felt comfortable about John, he would not have recruited him. He talked about the prejudices in the NFL yesterday and today. He compared the whites in the South to the ones in the North. He said that the Southern people were very open about their prejudices and the people in the North hid them. He commented on the meetings that he had with management in the NFL and how they talked so negatively about the black athlete. When it came down to recruiting an athlete, whether he was black or white, J.I. had one thing in mind. He wanted to utilize the athlete to win football games. He said that the color of a man's skin had nothing to do with how he recruited players.

He recruited John for his world-class speed. He knew that he could be used as a long distance threat. The dimensions of the football field in the Canadian League are 65 yards wide and 120 yards long with a 20-yard end-zone. So a wide receiver with great speed could be used in so many ways to offset the defense. This is especially true when one is on the one-yard line. A team has a longer field to run on with a 20 yard in-zone, and a man with excellent speed can be a great asset in terms of scoring touchdowns.

When John first came into the camp, J.I., the General Manager, made a bet with his head coach Sam Etcheverry that he could not out-throw John on the run. J.I. told me that his head coach didn't have much of an ego, but when he made the bet, it turned his ego on. They called John over and explained the bet to him, and John got turned on because he was a betting man. John was so confident that his new coach could not out-throw him that he lined himself in the backfield position rather than line up on the line of scrimmage. Coach Sam threw the ball, and John was waiting on it. Although Coach Sam lost the bet, he was amazed. In fact, J.I. was of the opinion that there was no one quarterback that could out-throw John. He said that this included Joe Namath, Johnny Unitas, and any other NFL or CFL quarterback.

The Alouettes had a strict policy that disciplined the team like no other team in the NFL or CFL. They did not allow Afros, white shoes, long hair, and they traveled to games dressed in suits. John did not have a problem with the dress code because most everyone dressed to kill in Harlem. J.I. told me a funny story about how John came to the airport for the first game away in Toronto. He wore a sweet gray pin-striped suit. He said that John looked like an English banker. But when the head coach saw him, he said to J.I., "Look at that son of a bitch. What is he, a clown?" J.I. broke out laughing, saying to himself, "What the hell are you talking about? Here you are wearing a Tyrolian hat with a feather in it, and you are going to say something about the way he dresses, looking like you look." He concluded by saying that John was dressed immaculately and Sam looked like a bum in comparison. So Coach Sam was the clown according to J.I..

John played one year for the Allouettes. J.I. explained that during the season the coach did not use John correctly on the field. Instead of throwing the long pass to him, they chose to throw him the short hard passes. It almost seemed that the coach wanted to get him hurt because the short passes allowed the middle linebackers a shot at him. John endured, but he was ineffective on the short run. I asked J.I. if he felt that the coach was prejudiced due to the way he played him. He said that he did not think so. It was a matter of not being smart in terms of using the player where he was best needed. Further, he said that his team, the Allouettes, was the only team to have a black assistant coach, Gene Gaines from UCLA. He also emphasized that the Allouettes was the only team to have two black quarterbacks during the time that it was not fashionable to have one. Additionally, he said that had the team kept John and trained him to play football, he would have been one of the best wide receivers ever. After a year, the team management decided to cut John from the team. A year later--in the 1971-72 season--he was drafted by Toronto's CFL team. They used him defensively as a corner back. He played for the Toronto Argonauts team for a year, and never returned to football again.

10

Back With The Olympics

Munich Olympics

In 1972 John resided in Montreal, Canada where Beconta, Inc., the Puma shoe distributors, contacted him. They asked him if he wanted to go to the '72 Munich Olympics to represent their company. It was a good financial opportunity, and an excellent way to see some of his fans again. So he said yes. In a couple of days he flew to San Francisco and talked to the management people about his job description.

John's job was to talk to the Olympic athletes and negotiate contracts between the athletes and the Puma Company to wear Puma products. At that time, sponsorship of athletic wear didn't bring the kind of revenue that it brings to the company to the athlete; money paid to an athlete was paid under the table. The contracts to represent at a track meet could bring an athlete $5,000 for participation. Today, the athletes get $100,000 or more, amateur or pro. John said, "The job was a Godsend. Anytime a man is down and out and there's no light at the end of the tunnel, when something comes along, it's a Godsend. God's been throwing things at me, keeping me afloat, despite the fact that so many people wanted me to fail."

When John arrived in Munich, Germany, for the 1972 Olympics, many people didn't expect to see him there. He talked to many of his old friends, and he made some new ones. He made connections to obtain seats for several people that he knew to get into the Olympic Games, like Jesse Owens and his family. All the German soldiers liked him and he didn't need credentials to go anywhere. The mayor of the village was a good friend of

John's too, and he allowed him to go back and forth through the village. He had access to all of the games.

One day, some foreign reporters wanted to take his picture. It was an unforgettable moment in his life. He explained it this way:

> I'll never forget it. The press asked me to wear blue pants and a cape. I was a little skeptical about the outfit, and I asked them not to print anything negative that would cause some controversy. They agreed. They had me to stand in front of all the Olympic flags in order to use them as a background. Then they asked me to stand at attention while I hold my hands on my hips with this cape on. I looked like the black Superman. They took several pictures, and sent me on my way. The next day, the picture was in the paper with a headline that read: "This Man Can Wreck the Olympic Games." The media took the picture and I never gave them a quote about anything. I made it perfectly clear to the press and the coaches that I was not there to cause any trouble; I was there to earn some money. Nonetheless the newspaper article expressed the fact that I could wreck the games with my running abilities, not my protest abilities. I really felt bad about the way in which the newspaper printed the article because from my experience with the white press, I knew that they would interpret it in a negative way. The white coaches from America would interpret the headline in a negative sense too. So I was

in a no-win situation. I tried to get in touch with the paper to have them retract the story, but that never happened.

Based on the fact that I was a celebrity, I got caught up in the swing of the Olympic games. I was a celebrity for two reasons. The first reason was the fact that I was a former Olympian, and secondly, I was a great runner. I was also a ladies' man. I had ladies all over the world, and that threw even more spice into the game.

ABC wanted to do an interview with John. He told them that he would be glad to do it if they were willing to pay him. They said that they did not have money to pay him, so he refused to do an interview. ABC didn't want to pay John, so they used a local station to trick him into doing an interview. John was training during that time, and the local press, which was foreign to him, asked if he would do an interview. He agreed to do it. So they sat down and recorded the interview; it went very well. At the end of it, just out of curiosity, John asked them what they were going to do with the material. They answered in their strong German accents, saying, "Oh, we are going to auction it off or we might give it to ABC." When they said that, he knew that ABC had set them up to do the interview.

John said he immediately became pissed off because of what they had done. They took the interview back to the studio. John was with a friend of his named Russ Rogers, a hurdler from Maryland University. John told him that he was going to go over to the ABC tent and find out what the hell was going on. There were several men in the tent, and the most noted one was

Howard Cosell. ABC had a gentleman by the name of Freddy Thompson, an attorney who represented ABC as their legal counsel. He was a former track star out of New York, and he understood the situation from an athlete's perspective. After John confronted ABC about the manner in which they handled the interview, ABC told him that they were going to show the interview and he could not do anything about it. Then Freddy Thompson, the attorney, told ABC that they would be liable if they showed the interview to the public. John looked at all of them and said, "I don't know who you guys think I am, but I didn't give my consent to anyone with ABC to do anything. Go ahead and do it if you want to, but in the end the interview will be called 'The John Carlos Wide World of Sports Interview'." Howard Cosell pulled John over to the side and stated that he would not allow ABC to do anything against John's will. John said that he would always have respect for Howard Cosell because he treated him with the utmost respect.

John's principal job with the Puma Shoe Co. was to do PR work with the Olympic athletes. He was instructed to convince the Olympians to wear and represent Puma Products. Art Simburg, the man who worked with Speed City, worked for Puma too. His job was to get the shoes and other products to and from different places in the Olympic area. John had been in line to receive the job that Art had, but after the demonstration, he was not worthy of the job in the eyes of the Puma Organization.

There was a misunderstanding between Art Simburg and his crew in terms of what John's job status was with Puma. Art apparently called the San Francisco office because he and his crew got upset when they saw John in a laid-back position doing PR work while they carried boxes of shoes around. Basically it was their job to make sure that the shoes and other Puma products arrived in the stadium. Once they arrived they distributed the products to the various athletes that accepted John's offer. The Puma staff confronted John, saying that along with the PR work, he was supposed to assist them with carrying the products. Refusing to carry shoes and other products, he told them that he was hired to do PR work and PR work only.

The management team in San Francisco sent word through Art Simburg that if he did not carry shoes like the other employees, he would not receive his pay. John rebelled by saying that he was abiding by the agreement that they made when he negotiated a verbal contract in San Francisco. The people from San Francisco called back to New York and had discussions with the Puma officials there. John said that Puma in New York tried to muscle him into carrying shoes around by making idle threats. He told them that that was not the agreement, and he wasn't going to do anything other than what was agreed. The situation got very ugly, and talks were broken off.

A few days later, Adidas' CEO Mike Lauraby was at the Olympic Stadium when John went over to ask to buy some of their products. Mike knew that John was a Puma man, so he thought he was joking. Then, John explained to him that he had a big falling out with Puma and they owed him money. His main concern was to purchase Adidas wear and sport it, so that Puma would understand that they did not own or make him. Mike and another associate, Haus Dashler, listened to John's dilemma. They were open to his suggestion in terms of coming over to their side.

John knew how to create a situation to bring on some competition. He challenged several sprinters in the village to race against him. It would be unofficial, and the winner would have bragging rights. Several athletes from around the world agreed to participate, but word got around to the Olympic Officials. They issued a warning to those who wanted to participate, saying that if they ran against John, they would lose their amateur status. This statement quickly nullified the race, and John was left hanging. Nonetheless, Haus asked John if he wanted to come and work for him. He replied yes! The Adidas Co. wanted to know how much the Puma Co. was paying the athletes so they could counter with a better offer. Well, the Puma Co. replaced John with a guy by the name of Russ Rogers. Russ didn't know what the situation was between John and Puma, and John used it to his advantage. He explained the situation to Russ. Then he convinced him to work as an agent for Adidas and Puma. All he had to do was give John information as to how much he was going to pay an athlete to wear Puma products, then John would come along and pay a higher rate to sway the athlete to wear Adidas. Russ was being paid to negotiate contracts by Puma, and John would pay him for the information with Adidas money. Thus both companies would pay Russ. So John would meet his objective to cut Puma off as pay back for not paying him.

The next day they met in Haus Dassler's Suite at the top of the Munich Holiday Inn around five o'clock in the morning. They had breakfast and discussed their strategy for the day. They got several athletes to wear

Adidas products, and the strategy was a success. They ran this operation for a few days, and John was satisfied with what they had done. John says that the Puma organization had done him a disservice, and he did what he did in order to earn money for his family and himself.

When it came down to getting the money that Puma owed him, John threatened them with a lawsuit. He said that the Puma employees threatened to wreck his marriage by saying that they were going to send information to his wife indicating that he was dating different women. The Puma employees saw different girls coming and going out of his room. John said that he wasn't taking different women to his room. The point of the matter was that he had five of his buddies who didn't have a place to stay. So he had shared the room with them. Some slept on the floor while the others slept on the couch. They also had a policy whereas the one who caught a woman first could have the room for a certain length of time. So several of the guys had girls going in and out of the room. The situation became very ugly, and he turned around and told the Puma people that he knew all of the people that they paid under the table since Jesse Owens. He also told them that if they did not pay him, he was going to go to the press with the story. Puma understood where he was coming from and they paid him for his services.

I worked for Puma when I ran track in high school. I worked my way up in the company. I told them from day one how to market their shoes. I was the one who took their shoe sales from five hundred to a million pair of shoes in sales. I had them make me shoes in various colors such as gold, red, blue, and other colors. I ran a race and afterwards I would take my shoes off and hold them up and kiss them to the crowd. After I took my shoes off, I autographed them, and I gave them to a fan. Puma pulled me aside and said that I gave away too many products. I explained to them that the cameras were following me every time I gave a pair of shoes away. I also articulated that as I traveled the world their products were being advertised.

In terms of new ideas, John asked Puma to use Velcro on shoes because he had seen how NASA had used it in the space program on the astronaut's equipment. He explained that it was better than laces. They took his advice and had good success with it. John had suggested that they make shoes for little babies and little people. They thought that the idea was ludicrous, but that became a million-dollar business in itself. He told them that they needed to sponsor a famous group like the Jackson 5 to branch away from sports. The Jackson 5 was seen all over the world, and it was possible that Puma could have made some shoes or outfits for them. They wouldn't listen to that suggestion until Boy George came along wearing outfits from the street.

John also told the Puma people that it was better to give than to receive. He said this because sometimes the athletes would come to different events and they would be in need of something and Puma could be the one to provide the need. John recalled on one occasion when Ralph Boston, an Olympic long jumper, was in need of a tape measure and Puma had them. Ralph was an Adidas man. They refused to give him a tape measure due to the fact that he did not wear their products. John, in turn, told them that Ralph was one of the greatest athletes in the world, and it was possible that Ralph would send them someone based on their generosity. John tried to teach them these principles, but they would not adhere to them.

After working for Puma in the Munich Olympics, John was let go. It would not be until four years later in the 1976 Olympics in Montreal, Canada, that he would have any contact with them. The president of Puma, Armand Gaster, had heard that John was in the area, and he sent one of his workers to contact him. The connection was made, and John found out that Mr. Gaster wanted to take him to dinner. They went to dinner, and Gaster began to tell John how sorry he was for the way in which his company had treated him. John said that Mr. Gaster expressed his concerns with tears in his eyes. He wanted John to return to his company, and work for him. He really needed help to get the athletes to wear his shoes.

John didn't know why, but he knew that white owners just didn't want to give black men any kind of power or position in their companies. He would always hear them say that they needed his services, but they couldn't give him any position. John told them that he would give them his services, but he couldn't follow their procedures. He had to get the job done John's way. They agreed! John took over the job that Art Simburg had had: paying athletes, getting the shoes to the athletes, and handling the contracts. John did all of those things, but Puma would not give him money to handle like Art got. When it came time to pay athletes, they would wire John the money.

He worked one year for Puma. Their ties were severed after John negotiated a contract with an Olympian athlete who in turn got a better deal with Adidas. The athlete returned to John indicating that he was offered a better deal. John told him that he was not locked in with him. He also told him that he would only ask that he give him a chance to ask Puma to match or beat the offer. Puma refused to deal and the athlete signed with Adidas. Puma was not satisfied with John so they let him go.

11

Family Matters

Tough Times

All these years John's family situation suffered tremendously. He traveled around the world making shoe endorsements, he ran amateur track, and he took odd jobs here and there. Neither John nor Tommy could find a good job. Tommy washed cars and worked other odd jobs too. John said that the only person to benefit from the protest was Harry Edwards.

Harry wrote a book called The Revolt of the Black Athlete. He placed a photo of the demonstration on the front cover, and the people bought them like hotcakes. He tried to make people think that he was there with us during the 1968 Olympic Games. He was not there! He was at home scared to death over the death threats that all of us were receiving. As I mentioned earlier, I talked to Harry about whether or not he was going to the Games. He told me that he was not going because of the threats. I told him that all of us had received them, and we were going there to Mexico to run in the open where we could be shot down. Harry became very wealthy from book sales and the fame that comes along with writing a book. As I said in the past, personally, I think that Harry is an opportunist.

Had it not been for his wife's excellent skills John and his family may not have remained together due to lack of finances. Karen always had a job, and she was the financial base for the kids when John was making the transition from one job to another. John spoke highly of Karen's education, beauty, motherhood, and her ability to put up with him. He encouraged me to interview his first-born daughter, Kimmy Carlos-Washington, in order to get a better perspective as to what kind of mother Karen had been to his kids. I spoke with Kimmy for almost two hours, and my interview proved to be most fruitful.

My mother was a strong black woman who believed in blackness. She came from a family that had a history that placed their roots in the Africa, the mother country. She let it be known to everyone that she was going to instill blackness into her children, and she was down for the cause for the black Power movement.

She was conscious of blackness at all times. In her world there was no such thing as good hair or bad hair. Nappy hair had just as much merit as straight. The extremely dark-skinned people were to be respected, and never spoken of negatively because America had brainwashed the masses to believe that the lighter skin was the acceptable beauty and dark skin wasn't. Black is beautiful!

My mother had beautiful straight fine hair that sparkled in the sun. But she was so adamant about the nappy look being beautiful that she either wore her hair short to hide the straightness of her hair or she grew it out and wore an Afro. All of the family members born to my mother's sisters have Arabic names. Every one of them was given a name that had meaning, and each child knows exactly what that name means. They identify totally with Africa: its language, culture, and religion. Since I am the first-born of the sisters, I do not have an Arabic name.

My mother taught my brother Malik Carlos and me to be independent. It was also imperative to my mother that I take care of Malik at home and at school. We learned to dress ourselves, cook, bathe, clean our rooms, and everything. My mother paid for me to take ballet lessons and other activities. She made time for us. But the one thing that I remember most is that my mother was not very affectionate with me. She seldom smiled; she seemed to be serious all the time. The only time I remember her smiling is when she asked me to dance for her. She would look at me and smile from the inside out. But as soon as the dance routine was over, she would say, "OK baby that's good." Then she would turn that smile off and be serious all over again. I love my mother very much, and all of the things that she taught me, I find myself teaching to my two children. She was a wonderful mother.

Kimmy talked about her dad in the same fashion with the exception that her daddy was very affectionate with her. She remembers every hug and kiss. She said that she was totally in love with him. And to this very day, John calls her his baby. So as you can see, John and Karen Carlos were great parents to their children, but they could not get things together for themselves.

Karen had high expectations for her marriage with John, but the problem was that she had to deal with the economic depression that came with the protest, hate mail, false information, photos of John with other women sent by the FBI, change of living quarters, promiscuity, and John being gone most of the year. She had a big responsibility to handle, and in time as you will see, she broke!

The FBI followed John's activities after the 1968 demonstration in Mexico. Their presence was obvious because he saw them everywhere he went. The first time that he noticed them, he kind of overlooked the situation. He was young, believing that he could do or take anything. He had never had any involvement with the government. Then, all of a sudden, the government was there watching his every move. He saw them morning, noon, and night. They tampered with his mail, and they did not keep it a secret. He imagined that when they opened it they said, "We opened your mail and we don't care if you don't like it."

John's friends from the entertainment world, track and field, football, baseball, and all areas of his life had to ask themselves whether or not they wanted to lose their economic base by associating with him. So most of his friends stayed away from him due to the pressure that the FBI and the government had placed on him. They stayed away because they felt that what happened to him could happen to them.

While John attended San Jose State in 1969, FBI agents followed him to the universities where he gave speeches. They took photos of him when he was around pretty women, and then they would blow the photos up and send them to his wife. They wrote letters that indicated that John had sex with certain girls in the photos.

In the early 70's, when his daughter Kimmy began school, it was very difficult for her to attend classes without hearing some negative remarks from teachers, students, and administration. John had to talk to her constantly to make her understand the situation. It was a very difficult task, but God helped him and his child to overcome the obstacles.

The economic pressure from the government was the thing that caused the most problems. John could not earn a living outside of hustling here and there. If and when he got a job it was minimal. Karen wasn't pleased with his activities based on the information that was coming in. The bills had to be paid; the children needed new clothes, food, and some of his time. Before the protest, John had earned lots of money and economically things were going well. They had everything that they wanted. But the game changed, and the pressure on him to feed his family was evident.

John's world was turning upside down. The pressures at home began to build to the point that he began to break down. He began to think that he was losing it mentally, and he began to get high and drink more and more. He wasn't being his old self, and life became a burden to him. He didn't want to face the day; he stayed in bed on many occasions while his wife went to work. The economic pressures from business and government had almost broken John Carlos! It got to the point that John's wife Karen despised him and he despised her. And at the same time they both despised what was happening to them. His wife, the children, and he himself were all confused. He put it this way: "You

266

could not call our family a dysfunctional family. We were beyond that because a dysfunctional family had a place to go for help. We had no place to go. Family separation was inevitable!" Around 1973, John and his wife Karen separated.

Women made it possible for me to provide for my family. I was able to pay my mortgage, bills, and buy nice things for my wife and kids. This was the only thing that I could do to survive. I had some conflict with what I was doing. I was not in love with all of those women, but I had a strong like for them. I also had fantasies about them that I fulfilled. I knew what I was doing was wrong because I had a wife. I had to face her everyday thinking about what I had done with the other women to pay the bills. My wife may have known what I was doing, and she may have become frustrated about it, and in turn she brought her frustrations upon me. I was in a wrong doing right situation. I was wrong for having different women for monetary gain, yet I was right because I was trying to provide for my family. I had to endure that situation, and God knows that it was not a pleasant thing.

I can recall on many occasions where I went to employers, and once they found out who I was they would have a different attitude. They would ask me if I was that person who participated in the protest in the Olympics. I responded, "Yes." Once they got confirmation that it was me for sure, they showed me that they really did not approve of what Tommy and I did. They refused to give me a chance at the job. The employers never took into consideration that I had a wife and children. I had discussed the fact that it was hard times due to what we had done. It was like revealing yourself, allowing them to know that you had a scar on your chest that's fresh, and then they take salt and throw it into the wound. Times got so hard until I had to question God as to why I had to suffer for doing the right thing. He revealed to me through His word that I had not done anything that He had not done in terms of suffering. We could have protested in other ways, but a silent protest was the most appropriate. For suffering is a good thing, according to the scriptures.

One day John decided to go see a psychiatrist. He told me that he spilled his guts out to her. She listened to him attentively, and her suggestion to him was to go on medication. But John didn't want to be prescribed drugs for his problems. What he needed was for someone to understand him and tell him that he was not crazy. Further, he wanted someone to tell him that he was not going to go crazy because of the things that were happening to him and his family.

The fact that John's wife had left him did not hit until one day he was sitting at home alone. He lived directly across the street from Pepperdine University in Los Angeles. He looked out of the window, and watched the students go in and out of their classrooms. On that particular day, it was storming with heavy rain, and the FBI agent that had been following him was sitting in front of his house in his car. John felt compelled to go out to him and invite him into the house. So he went out to the car and said, "Hey man, it is raining and cold out here, and I know that you have been following me so why don't you come in and have a cup of coffee with me?" The FBI agent said, "Man, I am almost retired, and that is against the rules, but there is no rule that says that you can't come out here and sit with me." So John agreed to his suggestion and went back into the house and made coffee for both of them.

He returned to the car with the coffee, and the agent and John began to talk. The agent began, "Regardless of what you think, the white agents, black agents, and others may not like what you did, but all of them respect the hell out of you." John was shocked when he heard those words come out of the agent's mouth. He said, "I can't begin to tell you how good that made me feel when he told me that. All I ever wanted was respect. I didn't care if an individual or group of persons didn't like me because it was all about respect. I had always given respect to people, and I demand it." John really got strength from what the agent had told him, and after they had finished talking, he went back to sit in the window to contemplate his life from the protest to that rainy day. After he sat there for a while, he came to the conclusion that his life was like a football game. The game of life was thirty-five to nothing, and it was the beginning of the second half. He said, "The game isn't over, it's the second half, and I am coming out to kick ass."

John and his wife went to court in a custody battle for the children. He said the judge was a "cold, hard, unconcerned ass hole." He took John's kids away from him! The case was decided not on what the facts were between him and his wife. The case was based on the fact that the judge knew who he was. He knew that John had been involved in the protest in the Mexico Olympics. He made it perfectly clear to everyone who was present in the courtroom that he knew it. The judge said these words to him; "I remember you and what you did. Thus, I am going to take your kids away from you." When he finished saying that, John lost it! He attempted to go towards the judge to try and get his hands on him, but John's attorney Al Moses restrained him. Al said, "I know that you are angry, but you will have to contain yourself." The bailiff, the prosecuting attorney, and Al Moses had to calm him down.

John calmed down and thought about what the judge had done to him. He said taking his children from him was like taking his heart and life away. He felt that America was doing this to him. He thought about all of the times he gave up to be with his children to run all over the world for America. John wore "Made in America" all over his chest, and he was proud! He thought about the money that the NCAA, Olympic Committee, and the universities earned off of him and of all the other athletes given two dollars a day to eat. They didn't allow them to earn money for their families to eat while the authorities ate like kings. There were so many things that crossed his mind, and he was not allowed to say anything in his defense because some judge decided that what he did was wrong. What an injustice this was to John, but he had to deal with it as he had dealt with all of the other negative things he had had to endure. John said that God works in miraculous ways because in about three weeks, his wife brought the kids to him saying that she did not want them anymore. He immediately took them to his home.

After about three weeks, his daughter Kimmy came to him and said, "Daddy, I want to go back to live with my mother. Daddy, it is not that I don't love you, it is that I need to go back to my mother because she needs me more than anything right now." He said that if he were stable he would have recognized that his wife needed some psychological help. He agreed to allow Kimmy to go to live with her mother, and immediately he awoke his son Malik to ask him what he wanted to do in terms of living with him or his mother. Malik said, "Daddy, I want to stay with you. I am tired of moving around, and I want to stay with you."

When Malik said that he wanted to stay with his dad, John forgot about everything because he was so happy. John went to court to get legal custody of his son because he did not want to have any problems in the future in case his wife changed her mind about wanting to take Malik. Nonetheless, his daughter returned to stay with her mother and his son stayed with him for a year. Karen got visiting rights and she took Malik on weekends. One day she decided that she would not return Malik to John. John had papers from the courts to legally have his son and when he went to the police, they told him that his papers were no good, because the court recognized him as the villain from the '68 Olympics.

John got pissed off and went to see an old friend by the name of Al Patton. He talked to Al about his situation, and Al told him that despite how he felt, he had the responsibility of taking care of his kids. Al also said that those were his kids, and even though their mother was fucking up, he was still responsible for their safety and well-being. He said that John had always been a man, so he should continue to be one by taking care of his children. John told him that he couldn't see giving Karen any money. Al told him to send money anyway, and keep all of the receipts. The advice that Al gave him was like a father to a son. It was excellent advice. In time, they had to go back to court.

Again, the judge awarded the children to his wife. John got visitation rights, and she could not leave the state or city without the court's permission. His wife left Los Angeles right after they had gone to court and went to San Jose, California. She survived by getting on social services. She also told the social services people that she did not know where John was, and they went for it. She stayed away for about two years, and he continued to send money to her for the children, keeping his receipts like Al had told him. John felt bad over the fact that he was not there to be with his children, but he thanked God that he was contributing to them financially. He kept in contact with his kids through his friends Jerry and Pooche Williams and Larry and Frances Gatson.

During that time John's sister Hepsy lived near, and when he came home from work, he saw a large box on his porch. The box was half wet from the rain. He looked inside of it, and noticed that it had clothes in it. The first thing that John thought about was his kids, and he panicked. So immediately he rushed over to his sister's house, and she met him at the door saying, "Don't worry, I have the kids here with me." John settled down, went inside, and grabbed both of his kids to hug and kiss them. And to his surprise, the kids were happy to see him. Hepsy had gotten things arranged so that he could continue to work and take care of the kids.

Karen had returned to Los Angeles. She applied for employment to work for the County Probation Office. He got information as to where her office was, and proceeded to go there. He went there specifically to ask her to write a letter to the judge specifying that she didn't want custody of the kids anymore. It didn't take long before she became angry and she stormed out of her office. She went out of the building to her car. John followed her. When he arrived at her car, she pulled a pistol on him.

It never dawned on John until later in life that his wife needed help by the way she acted in the office and in the car. But John needed help too, and when she pulled the pistol out on him saying, "I'm going to kill you," it was almost like he wanted her to shoot him. He said that he would never forget the expression on her face. Her eyes were eerie and strange. But he was so angry that he went into a rage, and went to hit her. He said that he tried to take her head off! So to keep him from hitting her, she rolled the window up quickly, and the punch that he threw went through the window directly to her head.

The rage frightened her to the point that she knew that she had to do one of two things. She either had to shoot him or leave the place in a hurry. She chose to leave. The people who worked in the probation department came out to see what was going on. Several of the workers saw the end result of the incident, and by the time the others got there, Kim had sped out of the parking lot. They assessed the situation, and they began to talk to John about the way his wife had been acting. He asked them why they did not give her some psychological help if they thought that she was acting strange.

They looked at John all strange, never giving him a straight answer. While all of this was going on, John thanked God that his kids did not have to see what had just happened; the people in the office were kind enough to keep them in the building while all of the commotion was going on. Afterwards John got the kids and left.

During the years of separation from his wife, John continued to get involved with other women. But there were two that were steady. For a while he dated a woman by the name of Debbie Renwick. John explained that Debbie understood his situation, and she helped him to pay his bills and other things. She stood by his side, being very loyal to him. He also dated another woman whose name I can't disclose. She was a business partner of his. The relationship began as purely platonic, but as time progressed, it turned into a love affair. She had a baby by him, Shana Carlos, who was born February 7, 1976. So from 1969 to 1981, John had different women in his life who offered to pay him to be with him for whatever reason they might have had.

John was still a ticket attraction for the amateur track and field associations. So he got himself involved with the Masters Track Meet in 1977. The Masters is an amateur association that ran all over the USA. He was a winner as usual, and he was selected to run in South Africa. At first John did not want to go because the Masters program wanted him to pay his own way. But things changed, and they decided to pay for everything. John knew what Apartheid was, and he wanted to see it first hand. He also wanted the blacks in Africa to know that other blacks were not afraid to come there and face Apartheid. He flew to Johannesburg, South Africa. From the start, John could identify with Johannesburg because it was a large metropolitan city like New York. Getting word that the Soweto Township was about 30 miles from Johannesburg, he decided to visit. So he rented a car and drove there. In contrast to the beautiful metropolitan Johannesburg, Soweto was totally impoverished with old shacks, trash everywhere, and people walking around in tattered clothes. John, having an open personality, began to talk to the people. He stood out because he was a free man. Once the South Africans found out that he was an American, they began to open up to him. Many of them knew about blacks in America and their struggle. John spent about a half a day riding around talking to different people to get as much information as he could about what was going on at the grass root level. Then he returned to Johannesburg to participate in the track and field events.

When he wasn't on the track, he wondered how differently the whites lived in Johannesburg versus Soweto. It was like night and day. In his quest to learn about South Africa, he ran into George Carlo, a hustler like John, who sold fake diamonds. He ran his game on John, explaining to him that he had some genuine diamonds for a cheap price. George didn't know that he had met his match because John used to handle diamonds at one time himself. So John asked George if he could look at the diamonds, and upon examining them he determined that they were fake. George was shocked! He could not believe that a brother from the USA could know his game. After George and John had discussions about the diamond trade, George asked John what his name was. When he said John Carlos, George knew who he was from the demonstration and track and field.

From that point on, John said that George treated him as if he were a god. George had a car, and he took John back and forth to Soweto. Both men were hustlers and drinkers. George took John to a house where they sold beer. They talked and drank, George constantly introducing him to the people in the township. In time, the word got around that John Carlos was in the township, and people all over came to talk to him. This is when discussions broke out about the real issues in South Africa. There were discussions about breaking down the color barriers where everyone, including the whites, had a social class. The social class was based on the color of the skin, white being at the top of the class down to the blackest of blacks which was the lowest. The whites had total control of the government, business, land, military, industry, and education. Blacks needed to have an ID on them at all times. If they didn't, they could suffer any punishment deemed necessary by the police or military, including death.

Women and men talked about how the men worked in the mines far away from their families, not being able to leave until they completed the job or got special permission. The workers were paid a thousand dollars a year to work the mines. Then the whites would hire snitches and pay them twelve hundred dollars a year to report any kind of unnecessary activities. The snitches made it very hard on the regular workers. John spoke to some of the snitches explaining that they were wrong and they should be helping not hurting the situation. There were cameras in the township that monitored everything. It seemed like a no-win situation for blacks in South Africa; if blacks and all South Africans weren't free, then no one was going to be free. This was the belief of the revolutionaries in South Africa. They were relentless!

After the track meet in Johannesburg John decided to have a party in his room at the Holiday Inn. He invited George and several other people from the township to the party. John said that they had a funky good time. They partied until 3:30 in the morning. When George returned to the parking lot where he parked his car, it was gone. He reported it to the police. Since he did not have a way to go home, John invited him to sleep in his room. The next day John received a call from the police while he was enjoying breakfast in the Holiday Inn restaurant. The police had made a mistake in identifying the car, thinking it was John's. The mix up was in the last names Carlo and Carlos. So John told the police that it was his car and he was going to come down and claim it.

The police who handled the case were these big black, robust, mean-looking cops who often dealt cruelly with blacks. When John and George made their way to the station the policemen stood with their guns and K-9 dogs. They weren't friendly at all. They told John that they found his car near a bridge, and the thieves who stole his car took the new tires that he had and replaced them with some used tires. John knew that the police had taken the tires by the way in which they told the story. Anybody with good sense knows that a thief does not replace anything. John got upset with the cops, and he told them that the story was bogus, and he believed that they took the tires. The police did not like his response, and they began to talk crazy to John. At the same time, John broke into his fighting position, squaring off with them. There was a big commotion, and the cops backed down because John told them that he was an American citizen and he did not give a fuck about their system. John eventually received the car for George and they left the station without any further confrontation.

Over the next several days, the Masters Track Team traveled to other cities in South Africa to compete. There was Durbin where the Indians from India lived, and the city of Victoria. Victoria had special meaning to John because he got a chance to use his influence to integrate the stadium for the first time. When it came time for the track and field event to begin, John told the white South Africans that he was not going to run if they did not allow blacks to enter and watch. The stadium in Victoria had large clean sections set aside for the whites to sit and watch the field. The other areas were dirty and unfit for others to sit. There were at least two thousand blacks looking through the gates trying to get a glimpse of John at the meet. The South African whites were hesitant about allowing the blacks to enter, but they wanted to see John run. So they agreed to allow the blacks to sit in the dirty section. The blacks that came in were ecstatic, John said. They cheered and screamed the whole time. They were happy for two reasons. The first reason was that they got into the stadium where they were not supposed to be. Secondly, they got a chance to see John run. John put on a show that day and everyone was satisfied.

Secretly, John made a quiet attempt to see Nelson Mandela. He tried to pull as many strings as possible, but to no avail. Nonetheless, the whole purpose of the trip was to see what Apartheid was all about.

After about two months in South Africa he stopped in Kenya and Nigeria, then decided to talk to the Puma people in Germany. They again hired John, sending him to Edmonton, Canada, to the Commonwealth Games. John had made a mistake by making a quote that got back to the Queen of England; when he was in Australia the press had asked him a question about England, and he said, " God bless the king, and screw the queen." The press printed the quote, and it got back to the Queen of England. She made note of it, and when John came to Edmonton with his credentials from the Puma company, his name was on the Queen's do not participate list. So the people who checked the credentials saw John's name and threw him out of the village. They mentioned the fact that they wanted to throw him out of the country, but he told them to back off because he was a citizen of Canada. He showed them his citizenship credentials and they backed off immediately.

John was outside the village when he was told that he had an emergency call from the United States. He went over to the Canadian Police booth at the village and asked them if he could call collect to the states. He told them who he was, and they allowed him to call Los Angeles. So John called and asked what had happened, and his sister told him that his wife had committed suicide. This was on August 1, 1977. John said, "You know it was the strangest thing because I was having so many problems with that woman that I had to ask God to do something about the problem." He had told God that if he didn't do something, John would. He was to the point that he would have hurt her himself. By the time he got the news and returned to the states, his wife had been dead for eight days. Her body had begun to deteriorate, and the funeral home did the best they could to maintain the body's integrity. After all the hell that he went

279

through with his wife, he found out how much he really loved her during the funeral.

He cried like a baby when he saw her lying in her coffin. His friends could not understand how he could express so much emotion for her after she had put him through so much. But John told them point blank that she was the mother of his children, and he didn't appreciate the fact that they would ask him about the manner in which he was responding to the death of his wife. He looked into the coffin and reflected back over the years when he first set eyes on her--when he had predicted that the first woman who walked out of the girl's locker room would be his wife--the birth of his daughter and son, the protest in Mexico, the FBI photos and letters, economic depression, his womanizing, the breakup, the court cases, and the love that he had for her deep in his heart. It was the end for them, but he had to continue to raise their children, and give them the best opportunity to be productive citizens.

12

Charlene

Better Times

In June 1977, John was working for Councilman David Cunningham of the 10th District in Los Angeles as an office aide. He took care of 10th district problems from street maintenance to political issues. He worked there for a number of years until he got confirmation from a letter he wrote to Peter Uberoth, the U.S. Olympic Committee President, about obtaining a position with the Olympic Committee in 1982. He became a youth coordinator, public relations person, community relations and a special aide to Peter Uberoth. He also ran the Olympic Torch in the city of Los Angeles, which hosted the 1984 Olympic Games.

John worked hard and played hard. He was single and he enjoyed LA's nightlife. He and his friend Tony used to go and dance at the Black Playboy Club. John had been running the ladies and kind of doing his thing here and there. Finally, he had gotten tired of that scene and he wanted to begin another family. This was really on his mind. One night when he was at the Black Playboy Club he saw this beautiful, sophisticated woman sitting at a table with a group of her friends. He couldn't take his eyes off of her. He walked over and asked her to dance. She said no! John refused to accept no for an answer, and he asked her why did she come to the club just to sit down and not dance. When he asked her name she responded, "Charlene."

In June 1999 I held an interesting interview with her. She was shy yet candid about telling me her background and how she met John.

I was born to James and Katie Sweney-Smith in Brookhaven, Mississippi. At a very early age my family and I moved to Los Angeles where I was raised. I attended my K-12 years in LA and I graduated from Manual Arts High School. After graduation, I enrolled at Trade Technical Engineering School where I earned an engineering certificate. I became an inspector for one of the first computer companies named AMDAHL. While working for the computer company, I earned a beautician's license to do hair. I also modeled professionally for several clothing companies. The most memorable job that I had was modeling for Creator's Playhouse, where I worked for three years. Chad White was the coordinator; we modeled African garments. I also played parts in Rudy Ray Moores' movies. I guess you can say that I have had three careers in my lifetime.

As far as meeting John, I met him at the Black Playboy Club in Los Angeles. I went there that night to console a friend named Kevin whose wife had just had a baby that was born with serious physical problems. Just as soon as we sat at our table John came over and asked me to dance. I said "No." He got smart with me and asked me why did I come to the club, if I did not want to dance. I felt that I did not have to explain anything to him, but he continued to harass me. My hair is very long, and on this particular night I had it styled up. My hair-stylist used a little red spray because he used me to advertise the salon where I worked.

John hit my hair saying that I had on a "punk rock wig." I never told him that it was not a wig. I allowed him to talk crazy to me. Then out of the blue, he asked me if he could buy me a drink. I told him that I did not drink alcohol. A really nice song came on and he left us to grab someone else to dance with. I told my friends that we better leave because he was a bit too rude.

I had a very bad temper at that time and I was tired from work. We walked out to the car leaving John on the dance floor. By the time we got out to the car, he was there in our face, with his glass of liquor in his hand. I asked him to return it because I knew the owner of the club. I did not want my friend to lose his liquor license because of him. John gave the glass to his friend Tony and he returned it. John asked me if he could take me to breakfast. I told him no because we had all come together. He said that he would take all of us out just to be with me. Again, I told him no. Over time as I tried to get into the car he would lean against the door, preventing me from getting in. During this ordeal, he asked me if I had any children. I told him yes, that I had two children. John had two Olympic pens in his shirt, and he said to me that the two pens were for my children.

Kevin and John got into it because he did not like the way John had been dealing with me. Kevin was around five feet seven and John stood six feet two inches. John was talking down to him saying that he was from New York and stuff. I finally got Kevin into the car and he said the dandiest thing. He said, "You know, there is something about him that I like." I said you mean to tell me after all of that arguing that you did with him you see something that you like. He said, "Yes." I said to myself whatever! So I gave John my business card and we left. I had relocated to Arizona due to a domestic situation with my man. At the same time, I worked in Los Angeles. I commuted.

When I returned to Arizona, I could not get John out of my mind. So I called back to LA to see if he had called. He didn't! I had planned to return to LA to live and so I returned there the next weekend. The next weekend arrived and I visited LA hoping to see John. I knew the club scene very well and I knew that he would not be at the Playboy Club. I guessed that he would be at the Pied Piper. When I arrived at the club, I walked in and saw John's friend Tony sitting at the bar. He called me over and I said to him that your friend did not call. He responded saying that John would be there shortly. All I wanted to do was give him a card, and I planned to leave. But Tony insisted that I stay until John arrived. He bought me a soda and in a matter of minutes he heard John's voice in the background. He said, "He's here." When John saw me, he pointed at me saying, "That's her." I walked over to him and I told him that since he did not call, I am giving you this card and twenty cents in case you don't have a dime to call. After I gave him the card and the twenty cents, I left.

The next day when I arrived to work, John was sitting in my shop. He was there every day for about a month. I did not know who he was as far as him being a world-class athlete. I thought that he was a bodyguard or something because he had real real attitude. But in time someone in my shop recognized him as the person who raised his fist in the 1968 Olympics. I wasn't into sports. I had heard about the event, but I never identified him with it. Eventually, he told me about it; I told my brothers about him, but they didn't believe it at first. So the next day they came over to the shop, and identified him for me. As months passed by, he took me out several times. He knew many important people, and he impressed me.

One day he came to my shop and he told me that he was going to run the Olympic torch into Manual Arts High School when the torch reached Los Angeles. I said "Hey, that is where I attended high school." I remember attending the ceremony. As John ran the torch, he recognized me amongst all the people. In fact, he stopped running and pointed the torch toward me. The press and the media were there and they recorded everything. They interviewed John, and the students will never forget the day that he ran through our school. My mother received several calls from friends and family. They asked her if I remembered the 1968 protest. She told them yes. The torch run was very interesting because when the protest happened my history teacher who was supposed to teach world history taught black history to us. When the protest happened, that teacher took us to the auditorium and lectured about what was going on.

John and I continued to date. I was also in a relationship with my children's daddy. He provided my children and me with everything. We did not want for nothing. I drove the best cars, my children and me dressed in the finest clothes, and we had two homes. I had a choice to make. I could either stay in an abusive relationship or get together with this angry man (John) with these kids. I took the angry man with the kids because every time I looked at John, I looked at my ideal guy. I saw everything that this man wanted to be. I saw him as a family man, and a man that really wanted to have things with me. I gave up the homes, my beauty shop, the Rolls Royce, the fine clothes and everything. A year and a half later, John proposed to me. In April 1985, we got married at Lake Tahoe where John had broken the world's record in the 200 meters. I had two children, Travion and Winsetta. John had three children: Kimmy, Malik, and Shana. He had a house in Altadena. When our families came together, the children had to make some adjustments, and financial problems arose.

John worked with the Olympic Committee. After the Olympic Games ended in October 1984, he was promised a job by Peter Uberoth and Mayor Tom Bradley. It never materialized. So he returned to the bottom of the economic pie again, searching for jobs that paid poor wages. This caused him to become bitter all over again because in 1977, he had had troubles maintaining work with his first family. This time he wasn't traveling around the world, leaving his troubles behind; he had to think about his situation every day with his new family. I was strong enough to take what he had to put down. I worked hard to help him to provide for our family.

I worked for a friend of mine named Claudette in Altadena. The name of the shop was "Pierre." Claudette taught me the ropes about the business. It gave me confidence to know that I could develop my own business when the time came around to doing it. When John worked on a job and the owners would find out who he was they would fire him right away. It seemed that they found out who he was around Christmas when we needed money the most. This happened so many times. Every time he lost his job I would see this look on his face that let me know that he had lost his job. The look was not a look of sadness; it was a look of determination and strength. When I saw that look, I fell more in love with him. I could always be myself with him. He saw the strength in me too. He fell more in love with me. He would say, "This is my type of woman. She is strong like me, a fighter." I stood my ground as a woman. His woman! We made it!

The business world would not forgive him for participating in the 1968 Mexico Olympic Protest. John and I argued and fought many rounds about finances, but we did not allow it to affect our love for each other. Our children did not suffer because of our financial burdens. He made things happen under the tough times. Things got better with time and we provided everything that our children needed. Although John was drinking with an attitude, we put our faith in God. We began to attend Saint Andrews Church where Rev. Tuson was the pastor. Our children sang in the choir and we were very much involved in church activities. It helped us tremendously.

In 1989, I took a trip with a friend named Michelle to Palm Springs to visit her daughter Tony at Angel View Hospital. John had a half-sister named Doris living in Palm Springs. Doris had a daughter named Precious. Precious told me that Palm Springs did not have a black beauty salon. The only one that she knew of was Eva's beauty shop in Indio. I thought about it and I continued to visit with my friend Michelle. One day John, the children, and I visited Doris. During the visit, John went to visit Sonny Bono. Sonny wanted John to come and work for him. We returned to Altadena, sold the house, and moved to Palm Springs. During the transition, Sonny Bono's people gave him information about John's activities and the job offer that Sonny promised was no longer available. We were determined to make it. We did a quick search and found a house, then I found a building and set up shop. My place of business is called Ms. Charlene.

I had made connections customer-wise through Doris and Michelle. I am a very friendly person and I began to tell my customers that John was in search of employment. I was informed that there was a security job position at Palm Springs High School (PSH). I told John about the job. He applied and got the position. As time progressed, he became an In School Suspension Supervisor (ISS). He also coached track and field. He has been working for PSH as an ISS supervisor to this very date, May 10, 1999.

Moving from the hustle and bustle of big city life to a resort town like Palm Springs would take some adjustments. Palm Springs is an Inland Empire city located in Riverside County's Greater Coachella Valley, known for two things: agriculture and golf. The Coachella Valley grows 880 million tons of fruit and vegetables every year feeding three quarters of the world with its produce. Coachella also has a billion dollar golf industry where the rich, famous, and the average working man or woman can golf. Employment opportunities are service-oriented. Population wise, the majority of people who live in Palm Springs are white or Mexican. The Indians own and rent much of the land. Lastly, Palm Springs is also known to be a very conservative town.

It seems almost ironic that John Carlos would consider living in a town that is so contrary to his personality and style. But John has been around the world and he has the ability to adapt to any situation. The students at Palm Springs High School, with whom he has established a great rapport, love him. They see him not only in person, but they see and read about him in their encyclopedias and history books. He not only counsels and supervises them; he is a friend. As far as the school administration is concerned, many do not like him due to the Olympic Protest. But life goes on.

When two people come together with children from prior marriages, the children are affected in many ways. John encouraged me to interview Kimmy, Malik, Shana, and Winsetta to see what their responses were to his marriage with Charlene and the way he raised them. When they got married Kimmy was 17 and one year away from leaving to go to college. Malik was 12. Trevion was 10, but he eventually moved in with his grandmother. He was murdered in Los Angeles in 1998. Shana was 6 and Winsetta 5 years old. Malik said:

> When my dad and my new mom got together, it was a new beginning for me. I remember what it was like being with my mom as a single parent and my dad. I wished that they could have been together, but it did not work that way. Charlene was the next best thing to my mother. She fit perfectly! As far as my father and Charlene coming together, my father became a new person. It was a new beginning for both of us. I met Charlene

before they got married and we did things as a family. So everything worked out well.

Both of them were very militant, and they had me read books about Dr. King, Malcolm X and other black leaders. When I got out of line, he spanked my ass. For example, if I did not clean my room, he made me write a paper about what duty and responsibility was. Sometimes my punishment would be to go to the library and study. He always had a story to tell me about life and how to deal with it. He kept me in line. I could not deviate from the norm.

Educationally, everything was a lesson or a speech. My dad taught me about the streets and what to look for. He said that women and partying would always be there. He reminded me constantly to get an education first and everything else would fall in place. He talked to me about attending a college or university. I was an A\B student. I did not play sports in high school because I did not want to miss anything.

When I graduated from John Muir High School in Pasadena I wanted to do something honorable. I joined the Marine Corp. Athletically speaking, I was ranked number one in my battalion. I played football for the Marine Corps and I got a chance to travel. Presently, I am training in Special Forces to become a Green Beret.

The star side of my father and his involvement with the Olympic Protest was noticeable right away. I can remember meeting many famous people. I recall seeing the media record interviews with him and then I would see my dad on TV. Then word got around at school as to who my father was. Several students wanted to come by my house to meet him. It got to be a little overwhelming to the point that I did not want to talk about his fame sometimes. I had a couple of incidents where people did not view my father in a positive light, but that did not stop anything because he will always be dad!

I wrote my dad a letter thanking him for disciplining me and assisting me to develop my personality and character to be a model citizen. I probably shocked him when I told him this, but I really appreciate him for being there.

My interview with Winsetta was short, but right on time. She was very honest about how she felt when she first met John:

When John and his kids moved in, I was the only child at home. Trevion had gone to live with my grandmother. Now I had to share time with three other people. I did not want John to discipline me because I felt that he was not my daddy. I did not get along with Shana, but Malik was cool. Kimmy was doing her own thing, and within a year she left. As time passed, Malik joined the military, Shana left, and I was the only child at home. My dad John and I became very close. I mean we developed an excellent relationship. I never had to deal with his celebrity status because I did not attend Palm Springs High. Secondly, my last name is Bell. The only people who knew that he was my dad were my immediate friends. To conclude, I must say that I am very pleased to have him as a dad and a very close friend.

Interviewed last was John's baby girl Shana.

As a child, my dad was a disciplinarian. I mean very strict! He laid his rules down and he expected me to follow them, and when it came down to choosing friends, he chose them. He said that education was the most important thing to think, to concentrate on, not worrying about friends. His strict discipline was an offense to me. I did not like it at all! I left home at the age of fifteen, and I did not understand where he was coming from until I became independent and on my own. Then, everything that he told me became a reality and I could appreciate the things he instilled in me.

Although I rebelled, I could not do anything negative without hearing his voice in the back of my head. And educationally speaking, I did not want to disappoint him. I had to at least graduate from high school on time, and though he has not said it out loud to me, I know that he is proud that I did. Overall, my dad has been a good dad, and I love him!

13

History Day Competition

Raymond Cree Champs

John really loves to be involved with helping students. In 1995, he was contacted by letter by Adam Borba, John Garmon, and Sean Buford, students from Raymond Cree Middle School in Palm Springs, California. Needing to do some interviews and some extensive research for the National History Day Competition, they had chosen him as their research model. After investigating the validity of the letter he gave them a definite "Yes."

Funded by the Department of Education, the National History Competition has been an annual event for 24 years. Each year, a governing body selects a theme and the students compete in seven different categories. The theme for the 1995 National History Day Competition was "Conflict and Compromise." This is a very broad theme, and students had the opportunity to choose a topic from local, national, or world history. The Raymond Cree students had a host of areas to choose a topic from, but they felt comfortable using someone from the community in which they lived. They chose to research John's story.

As Tommy Smith had participated in the Silent Protest in the 1968 Olympics they also tried to contact him to do an interview, but he never responded to their request; they were disappointed! John commented, "This 'no response' action is typical of Tommy. I pray that some day Tommy will humble himself. Nonetheless, the show must go on, and the students decided to use me as their model." Additionally, the students found some information on Dr. Harry Edwards, and they used it too in their research presentation.

There are two divisions in the competition. There is the junior high school division, which consists of grades six through eight, and the senior high school division for grades nine through twelve. Adam, John, and Sean were eighth graders, competing in the junior high school division. The competition begins at the local level. Schools compete against each other within their district, and two representatives from the junior and senior divisions are chosen from each category. The representatives then move on to the county competitions. The 30 counties in the state of California compete for a chance to send representatives to Sacramento for the state finals. Ultimately, the winners of the state finals go to the Nationals to compete at National History Day's Competition at the University of Maryland in College Park, Maryland.

The student competition lasts for an entire academic school year. The students are selected; they are given the rules of the competition; and they begin their quest to develop a title based on the annual theme. There are about 500,000 students that initially enter the competition. The entrants research their theme and choose their projects from categories, such as individual drama, multimedia group, individual research paper, etc. Adam, John, and Sean elected to compete in the category of multimedia group. The title of their presentation was, "Taking a Stand at the 1968 Olympics."

There are two reasons for having this competition. First, the students get an opportunity to involve themselves in educational research, where they are able to compete, travel, and learn from others in the process.

Second, the competition is to vie for scholarships. The students can earn an award ranging from $250 in cash to a full scholarship from Case Western University.

Soon, John received a call from Adam Borba, and he arranged a time and place to meet for the interviews. They met at the Raymond Cree Middle School on two occasions, which constituted around 10 hours of interview time.

During the well-run meeting the students asked prepared questions that encompassed John's whole life. They went through rounds and rounds of questions, the students using an antiquated tape recorder and speakers to record the sessions. Adam's mother took photos during the meeting.

John had to dig really deep into his memories to give them the substance they needed in order to understand where he was coming from. He told them many of his personal endeavors, and he seemed to astonish them. They were very kind and polite, and they absorbed every word that came out of his mouth. He made them laugh on many occasions and caused them to think about what it would be if they were black men in America. He not only touched their minds, he touched their souls, inspiring them to seek the truth, and determine whether or not he and Tommy were right or wrong for participating in a silent protest. Further he made them look into their own minds to see if they were genuine and open enough to assess white America, and determine whether or not it was right or wrong. Without doubt, they were pure and receptive to the truth, and once John understood their openness, he felt good about the whole thing.

John understood the fact that he conveyed the truth to them, and they saw where he was coming from.

He urged them to seek the truth and verify the things that he told them, and said that once they verified it, they would be able to make a powerful impact on their judges. There was a great responsibility lying in their hands, and John wanted to see them do well. He helped to set the tone and the foundation for their fact-finding, and it would be up to them to do the research according to the parameters that the competition set for them to follow. They spent hundreds of hours doing research in the library, preparing the audiotapes, and organizing their slide show. In all it took them 400 hours to complete the project.

John was informed of their progress in the local, county, state, and national competitions. It seemed that they went through each round with flying colors and each time they presented their multimedia presentation they got better and better. The competition reminded John of himself when he was training to win the 1969 NCAA Track and Field National Championship. He had trained harder than he ever had in the past, and the more he competed the better he got. John compared his situation with theirs. He knew that they were well versed in what they were doing, and he knew about the hard work that they did to research what he discussed with them. John had discerned their candidness and knew that they had the ability to articulate the message. So without a doubt he knew that they would win the Nationals once they got past the state finals. And when he heard the news about their winning the national title, he was not surprised.

The news of Raymond Cree's junior high students winning the nationals was broadcast on radio and TV news. In fact, their victory was announced on the radio several times. The radio and TV stations in the Coachella Valley broadcast heavily on the day of their return from the Nationals. John was asked to attend a celebration at the Palm Springs Airport on the night of their return. "When I arrived at the airport," John said, "the parents, teachers, staff, students, cheerleaders, the Raymond Cree Band, my biographer CD, news reporters, TV crews, and people from the community were there." John recorded two or three interviews with the press and mingled with the enthusiastic crowd that awaited our national champions. As the festivities went on, we found out through the airport personnel that there would be a flight delay. Many of the press people were on a schedule, and they could not stay around to record the event. Most of the press left while everyone else sat around and talked until the plane arrived. I took photos of the event while they waited. John's wife Charlene, daughter Winsetta, and grandson Shannon were there to celebrate with everyone. John was so happy that they participated.

After two hours had passed, the champions arrived. The band began to play, the cheerleaders cheered, and everyone in the airport terminal began to cheer and gather around the entrance where the champions would walk through. The anticipation of their arrival was high, and everyone could hardly wait to see them. There were conversations going on all around the arrival terminal entrance, and it seems that everyone wanted to see them first. John was ushered to the front of the crowd by a very nice police officer, and he knew from where he was standing the champs could see him. Everyone was prepared to send a message of love; the photographer, the camera people, the reporters, the band, the cheerleaders, the parents and everyone else were happy for their accomplishment. Finally, passengers began to walk through the glass door from the outside. Everyone who walked through the door was greeted with a thunderous cheer from the crowd, anxious with anticipation, who thought that it might be one of the champs. After about fifteen minutes, the crowd got what they were waiting for. The champs walked in one by one through the door. The crowd became ecstatic with jubilation and joy. They cheered until everyone was tired. The champs walked directly towards John, and he gave them big hugs. Everyone wanted a piece of them, and he obliged the rest of the group by encouraging the students to mingle with the crowd. The champs were tired from the long flight and the time change. One could see the tiredness in their faces; nonetheless, they enjoyed the moment.

It was imperative that the city of Palm Springs and the school district give those three young men the recognition that they were due. But as far as John Carlos is concerned, he is sure that many of the authorities were disappointed over the fact that their winning was based on what white America might call a negative symbol.

John put it this way:

Using one of the most controversial protests of the century was un-American to many of the administrators in the district. I say this because many of the teachers and administrators are from that era, and they still have not been purged from racist teachings. If those young men had won a national title using a white hero like George Washington or Thomas Jefferson, they would have been allowed to take their multimedia presentation and present it to the entire Palm Springs School District. Not only would they have been able to present it to their district, but also they would have been able to present it to other school districts as well. Additionally, I feel that Palm Springs and the school district would have made this thing a citywide event where schools, businesses, and other organizations would have gotten involved. The limited pomp and circumstance was a way of holding them up and playing me down.

To prove a point about what he is saying concerning the old generation versus the new, there is the example of the awards luncheon that the city of Palm Springs gave for the champs. I attended the affair along with the winners, the mayor, school officials, parents, the media, and a few people from the community. The banquet room was arranged in good taste, and the atmosphere was mellow. John sat at the table with Adam, Sean, and John. The mayor had a table with some other dignitaries, and there was seating for family and friends. The media was doing one-on-one interviews with the champions while others sat around and talked to one another before lunch was served.

Once everything got situated, one of the school officials got up and spoke about why we were there. The mayor of Palm Springs spoke, then one more school official. Afterwards, the awards were given to the recipients, then the school official spoke again and thanked every one for coming. She was about to close the ceremony in order to allow everyone to eat lunch. We must keep in mind that the theme of this whole event was centered on something that John had done almost thirty years ago, and the school officials that spoke (two women) acknowledged him as only being there. Neither of them asked John to address the group, and he knows without a doubt that 90% of the people who attended wanted to hear what he had to say. John was introduced and that was all. Everyone in the place looked around at each other, and finally someone spoke. It was Janine Paquette, a former Riverside County Sheriff. Janine said, "Don't you think that John Carlos should have a chance to speak? I certainly want to hear what he has to say." After Janine spoke, all of us said. "Yes, we sure do!"

So John got up and addressed the audience. He talked about the champs and his involvement with them. He captured the audience's imagination with words of wisdom and knowledge. He wanted them to know that despite what some of them thought about him, he was "somebody." After John spoke, the people applauded, for they were impressed with what he had had to say. The two school officials had showed their hand, and he was sure that they felt small after he spoke. John meant nothing to them, but to those three young men and others, he meant something very special, and neither they nor anyone else can take that away from them.

I am very proud of those kids, and I wish they could have gotten the kind of recognition that they deserve. It is too controversial for a conservative area like Palm Springs to touch it even though the champions (three beautiful white kids) proved to the nation without a doubt that what Tommy and I did was right.

As indicated, there were 500,000 students that participated, and out of that number, it boiled down to 16 participants. Three out of these 16 national winners won first place using John Carlos as their theme for their history project. That in itself says something. It says that this young generation is open to the truth, and the judges were receptive to what these wonderful individuals had to say about his involvement in the Mexico Olympics. And when one observes the competition, where a particular topic stood out among the entire nation the way that this one did, it could not have been a coincidence. It was an act of God told through those young contestants who expressed themselves with truth in a brilliant multimedia presentation, an excellent essay report, and an outstanding news commentary. The only disappointment for John was that no student of color asked to do a report on him, especially an African American.

John feels a deep appreciation to the three winning candidates who used him in their presentation for a National History Day event. He put it this way:

> Words cannot express how grateful I am and proud of the multimedia winners, Adam, Sean, and John from Raymond Cree Jr. High. Our friendship will last forever. Much love goes to Sarah Mast, the two-time winning essay writer from Redwood High School in Visalia, California. I pray that God will continue to bless and keep you enlightened to the truth. Last but not least, much love and admiration go to the boy genius news reporter and anchorman John Freeman, Topeka Collegiate, Topeka, Kansas. When I watched his distinguished news commentary, it brought tears of joy to my eyes. You have a talent that will someday be viewed by the world. All of you are number one!

14

Conclusion

John Speaks

John Carlos has always been a fighter. He has demonstrated these attributes from the time he attended New York's K-12 system to the present day. The Silent Protest that he and Tommy Smith demonstrated on the victory stand in the 1968 Mexico Olympics is still being discussed today. The imagery of that event depicts the "sixties" decade in American and world history. In fact, it is the sixth most memorable event of the 20th century. Protest and politics have been part of the Modern Olympics and will continue to be as long as there is evil and conflict in the world.

After John Carlos and I completed discussions about his life, I asked him how he wanted to end his story. He concluded:

There are little brush fires in our lives that we need to address: social issues, poverty, illiteracy, depression, drug addiction, child abuse, pollution, racism, and hunger. These are some of the things that John Carlos has been concerned with in his lifetime. I put my life on the line and faced many obstacles, like when it came down to standing up for children to allow them a chance to obtain a decent education. I am concerned about all of my brothers and sisters who are locked up in institutions where they represent the majority in prisons and a minority in America. I am concerned about the way blacks are being exploited in sports at colleges and universities. These institutions still continue to pimp them by allowing them to attend their schools as a trade for their athleticism. Many of these black athletes can't read and write and when their eligibility is up, the schools will drop them like a hot potato and bring the next black athlete in. It is the same old game just being played in a modern way. But I still try and keep myself fit in order to continue to educate the youth by doing public speaking. I take a stand against the ills in society wherever I go. Further, I applaud all those who step forward to make a positive change. I denounce those who do not. I have never been afraid to take a stand for what is right!

In 1999 Home Box Office (HBO) presented a documentary called *Fist of Freedom*. The movie gave a history about the 1968 Olympics. Before the movie was recorded, HBO contacted me by letter that had a contract in it. I refused to accept their offer because they refused to pay me my price to be interviewed. There were many negative things that were said about me in the movie. Lee Evans (400-meter Olympic Gold Medallist, 1968) said that John Carlos did not attend any meetings, that he did not march nor did he participate in anything that had to do with the movement. Additionally, Lee said that he asked Tommy Smith about my participation in the protest. Lee stated that Tommy told him that he told me to follow just what he did. There was a comment made by Steve Milner about me smoking weed in the stands. I have never smoked weed in the stands before any event! I work with high school kids every day, and that statement should have never been made. I have no reservation as to what people are saying, but I say that they need to back it up with appropriate evidence. As to the general public, no one should take anything the media and the press says at face value. They have distorted and committed character assassin on many people by portraying them as villains. There are seniors and middle-aged people who can attest to what I have done to make a difference. At the same time there are young people out there who know of me, but really don't know what I am all about. The things that have been mentioned in this book about my life are a testament to the fact that I have been involved in the movement all of my life.

My main goal is to remain healthy so that I can continue to talk to the young people about good morals and standards so that they can be productive citizens in society. It does not make any difference where an individual comes from. It can be from the worst ghetto in the world, but that should not cause any one to say that they can't make it. No man can stop you from succeeding if you are working from your mind, your heart, and most importantly your faith in God. Man can try and intimidate you, blow bridges up, but God has made many paths for you when you open up yourself to Him. The greatest thing that we as people have, whether one is a Protestant, Catholic, Jew, Muslim, Buddhist, is the mind. God also gave each person a talent to do things, but negatives like drugs and alcohol, family separation, economic oppression, racism, and other things have caused many of our youth to go astray and not look into their selves to nurture their talent(s). We have lost many to drive-by shootings, illiteracy, prisons and juvenile hall. With an opportunity, many of these young people could have been the ones who solve the problems of cancer, diabetes, Aids, small pox, baldness, muscular dystrophy, and other diseases. It is the responsibility of parents, teachers, mayors, principals, senators, governors, and the President to help these young people to fulfill their destiny. I found my way and I made my mark in life. So it is important for every person to not give up hope. Don't ever get to the point that you give up on life because you have been dealt a bad hand. As long as you have breath in your body you have a chance to do something positive with your life. God is a forgiving God, and if you trust in Him, you can do many wonderful things.

I want to mention Minister Farrahkan, a man who is on the front line. He doesn't just talk a good game; he plays a good game too. He is not a minister and activist looking for the limelight when cameramen are there to take a picture. He is there when others are at each other's throats. He is there to take care of the poor, hungry, homeless, drug addicts and people that the system tried to reform and could not. Whites and blacks alike have ridiculed him because he speaks out openly about the ills in America. He orchestrated the million-man march and he was denounced. I have not seen clergy in any religion that brought together one million people before nor since that time.

He challenged any man to debate the issues of the day, and no one took the challenge. No one would debate him because they are afraid that he is too clever for them. If a man is grounded in his beliefs, what does he have to lose through debate? Congressmen debate every day, and on many occasions after debate they go and have lunch. Why can't clergymen do the same? Dr. King had relationships with clergy from every walk of life. Why? Because he knew where he was coming from, and no one was going to turn him around.

Mohammed Ali was a great athlete and activist. He was stripped of his championship title without a proper trial through the legal system. As a youth, he was flamboyant, articulate, and a poet. He created controversy and he was willing to go to jail for his convictions. Today he is sick and can no longer use his special gifts to communicate. Now the media, press, athletic associations, and others who denounced him have decided to give him his just due. I am happy that many wonderful things are happening for him, but again I think that they responded too late.

I think about our African ancestors who were captured and packed in ships like sardines in a can, traveling two and a half months across the Middle Passage (The Atlantic Ocean). Only the strong survived because half the people were dead before the ships arrived in the New World. Black people built this country on free labor, and we have not been given our 40 acres and a mule with interest. Reparation discussions under the assembly bill HR 40 is on the books before Congress. I urge everyone who is in agreement with the passing of the bill HR 40 to please write, email, or call your Congressional representative and ask them what they are doing to help it to pass.

I have stated my claim in 1968 that the Olympic Committee, Amateur Athletic Association, and the NCAA were crooks. The media and the press are headlined today in 1999 with news conferences and articles explaining how men and women in these organizations are taking bribes for personal gain. The committee members have received scholarships for their children, expensive gifts, paid vacations, and millions of dollars to buy votes. The votes were used to buy the rights to have the Olympics in a particular country. This eliminated the poor countries all together because they could not compete to buy votes with countries like America, England, Japan, Australia, etc. This kind of activity didn't just begin. It began from the beginning. The truth will always surface above evil.

If we do not clean up the mess that is in society, and the United States has a race war, all of the world will go to hell based on the fact that America is the powder keg. The only thing that will save us from total destruction is God through Jesus Christ. I have made a statement that went down in history, and if I had to do it all over again, I would do it without hesitation. God bless!

John currently resides in Palm Springs, California and works at Palm Springs High School. He is a consultant for track and field, private youth counselor, and is available to do public speaking at K-12 schools, colleges, universities, social clubs, churches, fraternities, sororities, and youth organizations. John has a web site and email address.

His web page address is: www.johncarlos.com.

His email address is: jcarlos220@aol.com.

Straight-ahead!

PHOTOS OF EVENTS

John, Andrew, and Earl Jr.

John's first corporate meeting.

Mr. Carlos at work in his shoe repair shop.

Chapter 8 John and Lee Evans together in Paris

John's Photo Collage

Chapter 7 From left to right Karen Carlos, John Carlos, The Honorable Willie Brown, Denise Smith, Tommy Smith, television star Ivan Dixon (Hogan's Heroes), Lee Evans and Sun Reporter publisher Dr. Carlton B. Goodlett . Picture taken at Black Community Support of Smith and Carlos actions in Mexico City on the victory stand.

John Carlos and Ronnie Ray Smith

John Carlos

John and Charlene at the piano

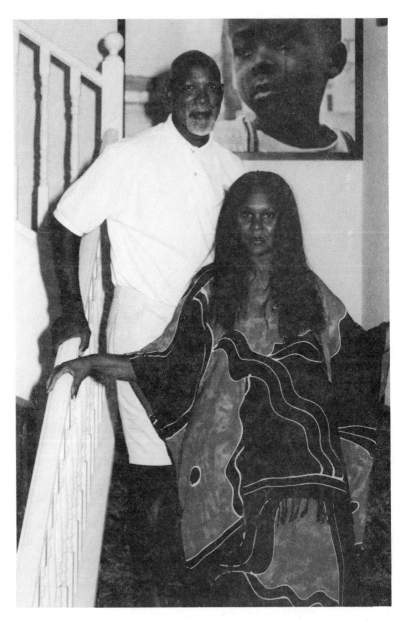

John and Charlene on their stairway

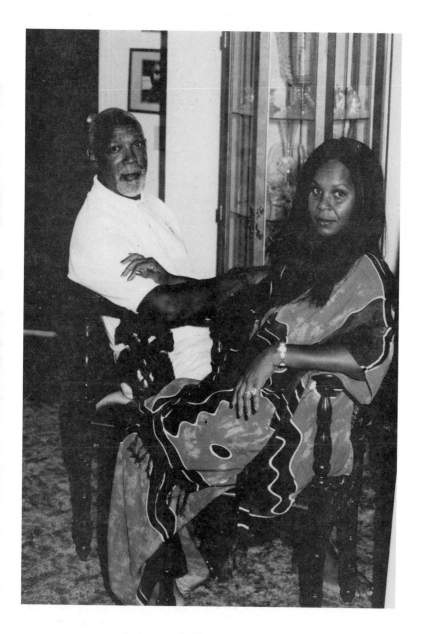

John and Charlene at home

John Garmon, Adam Borba and Sean Burford
National History Day Champions

John Garmon, Sean Burford, John Carlos and Adam Borba
Returning from the National History Day Championship in Palms
Springs, California.

CERTIFICATE IN LIEU OF LOST OR DESTROYED

DISCHARGE CERTIFICATE

OLER'S LICENSE ISSUED
August # 1932
WILLIAM A. BLAIR, County Clerk
ATLANTIC COUNTY, N. J.

To all Whom it May Concern:
Know ye, That

Earl V. Carlos, Army Serial No. *1869832* *Private* of *Headquarters Company, Three Hundred Seventy-first Infantry, United States Army*, who was *enlisted* in the *sixth* day of *November*, one thousand *nine* hundred and *seventeen*, at *Camp Jackson South Carolina* serve for the period of *the emergency* was **Honorably Discharged** from the service of the United States on the *eleventh* day of *March* one thousand *nine* hundred and *nineteen*, by reason of *demobilization*

This Certificate is given under the provisions of the Act of Congress approved July 1, 1902, to authorize the Secretary of War to furnish certificates in lieu of lost or destroyed discharges" to honorably discharged officers or enlisted men or their widows, upon evidence that the original discharge certificate has been lost or destroyed, and upon the condition imposed by said Act that this certificate shall not be accepted as a voucher for the payment of any claim against the United States for pay, bounty, or other allowances, or as evidence in any other case."

Given at the War Department, Washington, D. C., this *second day* day of *August*, one thousand nine hundred and *thirty-two*

By authority of the Secretary of War:

Adjutant General

Note.—This certificate is issued from the office of The Adjutant General of the Army without erasure. Any addition, alteration, or erasure made thereon is unauthorized.
W.D., A. G. O. Form No. 0150-2
April 21, 1930

Earl V. Carlos US Army Discharge Certificate

TRANSCRIPT FROM RECORD OF SERVICE.

Prior Service *None*

Battles, engagements, expeditions *Offensive: Meuse-Argo*
Defensive Sector: Verdun

Wounds received in action *September 28, 1918*

Decorations, service medals, citations, awarded *None*

Service overseas *France*
Sailed from U. S. *April 3, 1918*
Arrived at port on return to U. S. *December 29, 1918*
Character given on discharge *Very Good*
Certificate in Lieu of Lost or Destroyed Discharged Certificate previously issued in the
None
Remarks *None*.

Note: This certificate is issued from the office of The Adjutant General of the Army out erasure. Any addition, alteration or erasure made thereon is unauthorized.

Earl V. Carlos US Army Discharge Certificate

BOOK AVAILABLE THROUGH
Milligan Books
An Imprint Of Professional Business
Consulting Service
Why? $19.95

Order Form

Milligan Books
1425 West Manchester, Suite B,
Los Angeles, California 90047
(323) 750-3592

Mail Check or Money Order to:
Milligan Books

Name _____ Date _____

Address _____

City_____ State _____ Zip Code_____

Day telephone _____

Evening telephone_____

Book title _____

Number of books ordered ___ Total cost .... $ _____

Sales Taxes (CA Add 8.25%) .... $ _____

Shipping & Handling $3.55 per book .... $ _____

Total Amount Due...$ _____

• Check   • Money Order   Other Cards _____

• Visa   • Master Card   Expiration Date _____

Credit Card No. _____

Driver's License No. _____

Signature   Date